D1282286

# JUMP CUTS

## Snippets of my life in Television

### By
### Phyllis Ward

publisher

Phyllis Ward and Associates, INC

Onancock, VA 23417

© 2023 by Phyllis Ward

Kevin Stawieray Cover Artist

All rights reserved, published 2022

ISBN: 979-8-362891510

# To Michelle

# FORWARD

## noun: jumpcut

## (in film or television) an abrupt

## transition from one scene to another.

As my friend Moe says, "Is this going to be a long story?"

As my friend Richey says, "My life is a movie desperately in need of editing." Such wise words.

My life may have been different from yours in some ways—in others not. Likely I've had adventures you haven't. Television producing is like that. And the stories behind the stories—those are the real ones.

Some of these stories are just for fun, some sad, some about things you might not know. And many of them share hard-won life lessons that might be of use to you.

Here are snippets from my 25 years in television, in no particular order. That's why it's called JUMPCUTS, get it?

**Is this going to be a long story?**

**We shall see, Moe, we shall see.**

# MY FIRST DAY IN TELEVISION

## 1978

## MORNING:

Oh my, what a long time ago. Seeing **Patrick Duffy** in People Magazine, talking about his new romance with HAPPY DAYS actress Linda Purl...well I decided to write our story, his and mine. Most of you don't even know who he is I bet. When we met at the amusement park in Cincinnati on a summer day in 1978 Patrick was playing Bobby Ewing on DALLAS and at the peak of his fame. BIG BIG star. I was a brand-new intern at WKRC-TV and arrived just in time to help out.

On this day, Dinah Shore, American institution, was broadcasting her show from the amusement park and it was all-hands-on-deck.

Here is what Wikipedia says about her for those of you who have no idea what an American institution Dinah was:

**DINAH SHORE** (born **Fannye Rose Shore**; February 29, 1916 – February 24, 1994) was an American singer, actress, and television personality, and the top-charting female vocalist of the 1940s. She rose to prominence as a recording artist during the Big Band era. She achieved even greater success a decade later, in television, mainly as the host of a series of variety programs for the Chevrolet automobile company.

Wowee. Think I'm gonna like this TV biz.

Dinah's other guests that day were:

## THE TEMPTATIONS

Their hit "My Girl" was my favorite.

And

# NANCY LOPEZ

The young golfer making waves that year.
Nancy went on to become one of the greats.

At the pre-production meeting early, early in the day, the producers divvied up the tasks. I was the extra hand, of course. My immediate job was to ferry guests and other VIPS from the set to their limos waiting at the edge of the parking lot. Then later that night, after the show, I was to give the stars a tour of the historic inn where they were staying, just across the eight-lane expressway at the edge of the amusement park.

Easy peasy.

Easy enough for a while, but the park's 364 acres got confusing. The stage was closed to visitors, and it was easy enough to find, but which path led to that damn parking lot with the limos? I'd fumble the cart out to the lot where we could eyeball the limos…they were never very far away… and I always acted like I knew exactly what I was doing. Born producer, huh? Ha!

A bunch of the minor star minders got delivered to the bus that took people over the highway to the Inn, some bitching loudly that they weren't limo-worthy. My, my. But in general, my job seemed to be going well. As time dragged on, I got better at finding the limos. And of course, there were fewer. By the time I picked up Mr. Duffy late in the morning, the production assistant told me he was my last ride. Cool beans. But no limo. I repeat. No. Damn. Limo. Long before cell phones, of course, back in dark ages.. And I was waaay too lowly to have a pager. Round that parking lot Patrick and I circled. At least 30 minutes.

He was tired. And grumpy and wanted to get to his room at the inn. I sooo wanted him there. Need I add it was impossible to drive a golf cart over an eight-lane freeway?

Or walk.

We were good and truly stuck.

Twenty minutes later, I suggested he hop on the parking lot bus that pulled up to take staff across the highway to the inn. Not star-worthy, but hey.

ABSOLUTELY NOT!! says Patrick. We continue to circle.

Fifteen minutes later Patrick relents. Just get me out of here! We chase down a bus, he glares at me and hops on.

Whew, I think as the doors close, this TV stuff is stressful.

# EVENING:
# NEARBY HISTORIC INN ON OTHER SIDE
# OF FREEWAY

Throughout its more than 215-year history, the Golden Lamb has hosted, entertained, and provided lodging for many notable guests, including 12 U.S. presidents; political figures Barbara Bush, Mitt Romney, and Henry Clay; American legends Neil Armstrong and Annie Oakley; literary greats Charles Dickens, Harriet Beecher Stowe, Alex Haley, James Whitcomb Riley, Louis Bromfield and Samuel Clemens (Mark Twain); and movie star Charles Laughton.

I arrive all bouncy for dinner around 7:30. Me, basking in the glory of my quick thinking, getting Patrick on that bus. Ready to give my tour of the inn as previously planned.

Heads swivel as I enter—Dinah, the Temptations (one and all), Nancy, Patrick, my new bosses at WKRC and assorted hangers on.

**"THE BUS DID NOT GO TO THE INN, PHYLLIS!"** Patrick proclaims to one and all. "It drove in circles around the parking lot dropping people at their cars. Did you hear me, PHYLLIS? It did not come to the inn."

**"Oh Patrick."** Oh Phyllis. Oh FUCK.

To this day I have no idea how Patrick got to the inn. I apologized.

My new boss wisely suggested I give the man his space.

I spent dinner studying up on the inn's history and getting ready for my tour. Which nobody, especially me, had any interest in, but I guess we got special rates if the stars looked around.

So around 11 or so I led a tipsy group from floor to floor, opening doors and telling tall tales about Mark Twain and Charles Dickens. They trailed behind me dutifully poking their heads through the open doors, sipping their bourbons... next!

**The last room was the best.**

JOHN QUINCY ADAMS slept here (says the sign on the door)

…I said as excitedly as I could muster as I opened it with a flourish.

Behind me, peering over my shoulder, were Patrick, The Temptations (that would be Louis Price, Otis Williams, Glenn Leonard, Richard Street, and Melvin Franklin), Nancy Lopez, and Dinah, in that order.

Looking up from the bed was a startled couple, startled and stark naked.

The moment is frozen exactly that way in my memory. A flashbulb memory, they call it.

Everyone laughed. What else could anyone do? WRONG ROOM, I said and slammed the door shut.

It was sooooo unlikely a scene that all we could do was laugh. I mean, come on.

We wandered back down to the bar, and everyone talked about what a dunderhead I was.

Maybe worth keeping around just for the entertainment.

I have no idea who that couple was and if anyone ever believed them when they told their story. Surrrrreeeee Sam.... Suuurrrreeee... Susie...that's what happened. Suuurrrrreeee.

**I have no idea whatsoever why I ever had a DAY TWO in television.**

**Maybe it was just too funny.**

# RANDOM SHOOTS I'VE KNOWN

I **DID** have a day two, and three, and four. Full time for over 25 years, full of adventures and incredibly varied stories. Stupid and sublime, groundbreaking and ridiculous. Important, sad, and silly. Here is a sampling, in no particular order:

## "THANKS FOR THE USE OF THE HALL," AS THEY SAY

ADITI Festival of India…Ghosts of the Tower of London…Madame Tussauds in London…Plastic Surgery for French Women in Tahiti…Bali Hai Boys of Morea…Gauguin Museum in Tahiti…Agoraphobia…Ice diving…Motocross… Kids with Cancer…Maasai tribe in Kenya…Snake handler in Kenya…Laughing Baby Chimp… Documentary Golden Hour in Trauma Care … Giraffes in Kenya…Gurners in Scotland…Stonehenge…Castles in Ireland and England…

Ballooning over the Serengeti...Landon Jones (who invented the word babyboom)...Neputa Festival in Japan...Tea ceremony in Japan...Sword factory in Japan...obsessive compulsive disorder ...Dr. Fred Berlin  Child Molesters, Johns Hopkins...Psychic in Nairobi, Kenya...Night train to Mombasa...Migration of the wildebeests...New York City Comedy Clubs ...Diamond District, New York City...Eileen Ford Models...Past life Regression therapy 20/20...Jousting in England...Dude ranch...Rodeo...Patch Adams, Clown Doctor who started a movement...52 year old mom gives birth with daughter's egg... Cathy Guiswhite cartoonist...ASSIGNMENT DISCOVERY series  for The Discovery Channel...TEACHER TV series for TLC  Many seasons of shows for teachers highlighting best practices on subjects like: brain plasticity... Native Americans  sharing  their culture and language...

student centered learning…inclusion… and older students helping younger students…Undercover investigation of psychiatric wards in Mexico… Old hippies living at The Farm in Tennessee…Terrible conditions at border settlements between US and Mexico…Pat Choate—futurist…Dr. Ben Carson, performing hemispherectomies on children…Chuck Yaeger, astronaut…John Glenn, astronaut…Sally Ride, astronaut…Life on an aircraft carrier…Amish life…TJ Monroe, Disability Rights activist…Dolphin rape of women swimming with them (one of my favorites)…I Was Captured By An Alien—many of these—always in rural area…Loneliness of a Broken Heart…Waco Texas, FBI Sharpshooter… FBI training facility, Quantico, VA…Warthogs in Kenya…Assateague, Virginia pony swim…FAO Schwartz toy store in NYC…Gulf and Western cigar guy…Behind closed doors at the US Post Office and many more closed doors…US Coast Guard…ADA interview with President George H. Bush…Trial and Error- Hepatitis C trial gone wrong

20/20...Student Safari series for Discovery...Lunchbox Heroes Westinghouse documentary...The Wrong Stuff Documentary...TMJ investigation, 20/20...Does your Doctor Really Care? 20/20... Kids Who Rape, Breaking the Silence, STREET STORIES, CBS...Boxer Sugar Ray Leonard... Is it a Boy or a Girl? Intersex documentary, Discovery...Leprosy Documentary Discover... Three Mile Island, 15 years later... YOU ASKED FOR IT, syndication...SIGHTINGS, syndication... ENTERTAINMENT TONIGHT, syndication... Actors Fess Parker, Walter Mattheu, Judith Light, Alex Baldwin, Merlin Olsen, Tim Robbins, Kathleen Turner, Leslie Nielson, Brooke Hayward, Christine Ferrare... Katterskill Falls about painter Thomas Cole, Smithsonian... Baby Snatchers 20/20... Culinary Institute of America...Musician Pete Seeger...Spelunking...HOT PLANET Doc on Global Warming, The Weather Channel

And the fun goes on…

# NOTES FROM THE FIELD
# CREW STORIES

---My first day at a **paying** job in television I went immediately to the person generally considered the best producer and asked, "What's the secret of producing?" "Always feed your crew," she said. As I soon found out, there is nothing grumpier or less cooperative than a hungry crew. Nothing. Wise words.

---"Hi, I'm Phyllis," I say. "I'm the new producer. Nice to meet you Mr. Cameraman." He looks at me and says, "Producers are as useless as tits on a bull." Nice to meet you too.

Soon I was traveling the world and that very often meant a new pick-up crew every few days. Meeting strange, jaded men (in those days they were always men) who barely deigned to look at you, much less remember your name. Pretty sure this is when I started saying fuck a lot. It helped.

**Footnote:** All these years later I went to the nurse practitioner last week about my sore palm. She said it was a ganglion cyst caused by an overworked tendon on my right hand. Guess which finger?

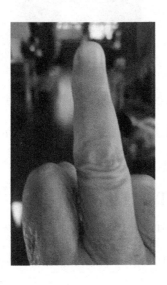

---Over time, it became clear I had to immediately assert my authority with a new crew. This joke helped: "So, a man walks into an elevator and sees a beautiful woman. The door closes and they are alone. He turns to her and says, "Can I smell your pussy?" "Absolutely not!" she says. "Oh, then it must be your feet."

I shared it soon after meeting new crew guys. They treated me much better after hearing it. Kinda sad huh?

In the picture above my favorite American crew, Craig (L-sound) and Gino (R-camera) are reminding me they are about to go into golden time---super, super overtime. No need to say it out loud of course. Or maybe they're just hungry.

They were the best. We worked together for decades.

**English crews are different.**

Television in England came out of the film tradition and so they had a lighting cameraman, an oh-so-serious sound technician, and a gaffer (lighting person) on every shoot. To record simple voice-overs on the road, mattresses were gathered from adjoining hotel rooms to muffle the sound. Unlike the Brits, American television came out of radio.

Basically, Americans added a camera to their radio mics. No gaffer. The English considered our standards lax. (Favorite American joke: How can you tell when a soundman is dead? He drops his donut.)

Luckily both American and English crews knew how to have fun. And all of us worked hard.

I told you mine was bigger...

For over a year I was lucky enough to travel with Peter and Bobby and John, former BBC crew mates who were now freelancing. Picture notwithstanding, they took their jobs seriously.

John Brown was our gaffer.

That's John on the left with me and a Maasai laibon in Kenya.

John is famous for at least two stories.

---First, was about the day TV crews were at the palace setting up to cover an announcement by the Queen. John was upset about the annoying sound of the simultaneous translation by the Japanese reporter. John slowly lured him into a corner closet, hidden from view, just as Queen Elizabeth arrives. The Queen begins her remarks, stops, and listens for the murmur she thinks she just heard. Nothing. Tries again. Again, it stops. Repeat. She slowly walks toward the noise and then throws open the door to the closet finding the Japanese reporter huddled in the corner, sitting on the floor. The press corps goes wild with delight and a good laugh was had by all.

Even decades later, when John went to the palace for a shoot, the Queen would greet him: "Oh, you're the chap that put that poor Japanese man in the closet." Nearness to greatness indeed.

---My favorite crew story of all time is also a John Brown story. Long ago when he was on staff with the BBC he often worked with the same reporter, lighting cameraman, and soundman. One day they were sent to cover breaking news at the prime minister's country home, Chequers.

These guys had worked together for many years and in the way of crews loved each other very much. When they arrived at the house and started setting up the cameraman realized he hadn't brought the camera. Wwwhhhaaaa?

No time to go back. London was an hour away. Two hours round trip.

This was a full-blown catastrophe. The cameraman would be fired. No question. Maybe in America he could find mercy but not at the BBC. No way.

And then John had an idea.

"Maybe the prime minister won't notice," he said.

"Won't notice?"

They put up every light John had, shining them directly into the prime minister's eyes. The cameraman hovered over an empty tripod; the reporter blocked the prime minister's view as much as he could. Whenever the prime minister looked up John hit him in the face with two sun guns (portable lights designed for spot illumination).

After what seemed like endless minutes the prime minister stopped the interview saying "So sorry chaps, don't know what it is with the lights today. I just have to stop."

The four of them went back to the BBC and said the camera broke.

John says the boss was beyond cheesed off. That's English for pissed, apparently. But nobody got fired.

**Now THAT is... Hmmmm... Loyalty?**

**Love? Stupidity?**

**Pure dumb luck? Maybe all of the above.**

# ONE OF A SERIES OF SOUVENIR STORIES

## "Christine at the Blackboard"

10x14 oil painting on my sunporch wall

**THREE FACES OF EVE** is a movie about a woman with three distinct personalities—Eve White is a timid wife and mother beset with migraines and blackouts. Eve Black is a party girl. And then there's the relatively stable and much more sensible Jane. The plot follows the psychiatrist who eventually helps Eve integrate these three personalities, allowing her to get on with her life.

Joanne Woodward won an Oscar for her portrayal, and it's always been one of my favourites.

Ah, but the real-life story is even more unlikely. The real Eve is a suburban matron named Christine Sizemore who lives with her husband in a modest suburb of Washington, DC. I am in her home to direct a television magazine segment about what really happened.

As usual, I'm feeling overwhelmed by the treadmill of two stories a week—find them, shoot them, write them, edit them, repeat. I'm told it's not a lot to expect, but decades later I am still undone. I can't do this, I will do this, no one can do this, no, it's only me who can't do this. Repeat.

Oh, shut up.

Sitting on the plaid couch in her family room, Chris tells me she actually had twenty-two personalities, not three. The baby, the turtle lady, the virgin, the whore, the purple lady (who, as I remember, only ate banana splits), the athlete, the man, the angry teen, the seven-year-old... it went on and on. Way too many for a movie plot, but there you go.

We sit side by side, looking at home movies of Chris transitioning from one personality to another. These mesmerizing scenes were filmed by her psychiatrist to help Chris grasp the tricks her mind was playing.

The black and white film is scratchy. There's Chris in a 50s' party dress— you know, the ones with the crinoline slips. You can hear the doctor's voice off camera asking to talk to a particular personality. I watch as Chris puts her head down for ten seconds or so and emerges as a new person, literally transforming before my eyes. Each personality has its own voice, its own posture, and of course its own eccentricities.

Good acting, you might say. Okay, but as I watch Chris transition from teenage boy to flirtatious bride, I can actually see angry welts appear on her arms. This new personality is allergic to strawberries, the one just abandoned isn't. That strawberry shortcake is now having its way. Hmmm.

In the film Eve is cured. In real life Christine still struggles.

"Sometimes I'm driving," Chris tells me, "And I find myself unexpectedly transitioning into a person who can't drive at all." *Huh?* She steers to the side of the road she says and calls her husband to pick her up.

"The first time it happened," Don tells me, "Chris was on the (Washington DC) beltway. Scary as hell. I tell her to stay off the damn thing. She's pretty good about it unless one of those teenage boys is at the wheel."

The placid calm of these descriptions makes me screech, internally. I am, after all, a television professional. My calm exterior, "Oh how interesting, Chris, do go on," and the internal one shouting,

"Are you out of your mind? Driving on the beltway?"

Well, yes, she is out of her mind. That's why I'm here. How and why did this happen? Her doctor's theory is childhood trauma. Chris's beloved grandmother died when she was six. Family custom required even little girls to kiss grandma in her casket. That terror, her doctor believes, led to Chris's initial "splitting off."

And then, in just a three-month period, Chris's mom cut her hand with a piece of glass. Blood everywhere. Then she saw a drowned man being dragged from a ditch. "Oh, and I saw a terrible accident at the sawmill," Chris tells me. "The man was a friend of my father's. He caught the blade wrong, and we watched him get sawed into three pieces. That probably didn't help either."

It was, I have to say, a startling afternoon.

Chris, it seems, shattered to protect herself.

It took most of her life to gather her 22 pieces back under one roof. Me, I did just the opposite, spending those same decades learning to let loose. Normal, well, NORMAL is a tough concept. And don't get me started on TRUTH. That doesn't explain the strawberry welts, though.

After the cameras left, Chris showed me her art studio. She had recently started painting scenes from her childhood.

The portrait she gave me, of Chris writing her name on her first-grade chalkboard—well, it's a workaday piece of art, but a treasured memento. "I wrote my name over and over," Chris says, "to hang onto myself. My name is Christine. My name is Christine."

**Whenever I doubt who I am in the world (that would be constantly) I sit on the sun porch, look at my small painting and get over myself.**

# FACTOIDS I LOVE
# THE SIX SECOND HUG

**TV research brought me this factoid**

This is the best factoid of all time. I use it every day.

As many times a day as I can manage.

Hugs have always been lovely but when I found out they feel even better if you hold them for 6 to 8 seconds, well, it was life changing.

An article from the UK's Daily Mail suggests "regular embraces can lower the risk of heart disease, combat stress and fatigue, boost the immune system, lower blood pressure, fight infection and ease depression."

Go ahead, try it.

Find your baby or your partner, or the next friend you see. Not the UPS guy. Too weird.

And make them real seconds. One thousand one, one thousand two, one thousand three, one thousand four, one thousand five, one thousand six. Eight seconds is better, but six is fine

Feel it? It's a real connection that opens up your hearts to each other. True science apparently, but it feels like magic.

**You're welcome.**

# BE CAREFUL
# WHAT YOU WISH FOR

Here we are, with the Publishers Clearing House crew, way too early in the morning, crouched in our rental van ass to elbow with the PCH rental van in front of us, in a far suburb of Boston. Waiting for signs of life in the house around the corner.

People in pajamas are now peeking out upstairs windows of the house we are actually parked in front of, the one down the block and around the corner from the house we care about. Upstairs lights flick on as someone moves room to room...Oh oh.

Here in our van, cameraman and soundman are grumpy. Oh joy.

This was supposed to be a quick trip. Up and back from DC in one day. Join the Publishers Clearing House Prize Patrol as they surprise a lucky winner. Fun.

These patrol guys have been surprising people for a long time and have it down to a science. Come into town, buy some balloons, grocery store red roses, and cheap champagne. Slap the flimsy posters that say Publishers Clearing House Prize Patrol on the rental van and go to it. (Flimsy, I say. This is so low rent. My illusions are shattering.)

Then proceed to the winners' house, hide nearby until the winners are at home. Knock on the door with an oversized winner's check and record the excitement. We follow the prize patrol to the corner deli to get the cheap champagne—they learned long ago that the expensive stuff was wasted on the average winner, who never drinks champagne and won't know the difference.

Most winners are of modest means, they say. The guy in line ahead of us is joking with the woman at checkout, saying he heard the prize patrol was in town and maybe he will be the winner. Everyone laughs. Now loaded up, the patrol slaps the sign on the sides of the van. We drive a few blocks to the winner's house, hoping to get this happy surprise over with and on camera.

As you can see Publishers Clearinghouse always brings their own crew to record the event for commercials. We are doing a behind-the-scenes. I honestly don't remember who hired us or if it was one of my bright ideas for a doc segment.

The afternoon light is fading, and no one is home. Darn it. Can't surprise people in the dark, cameras need light. Eventually we give up and resign ourselves to spending the night here in a cheap motel, with Burger King dinners and grumpy people. Oh, go to bed.

Waiting for an early start before sunrise to try again.

## DAY TWO

Once again, here we are, way too early, perched in tandem on the side street, waiting for signs of life in the house around the corner.

Neighbors are now gazing down at the van in front, the one that says they won!

"YES, it's those people. It is! It's us! We won!"

But we aren't coming to your house. Sorry. It's the one around the corner.

And now a second house across the street is taking notice. ...Oh oh.

Still no sign of life around the corner, but time to move. In tandem we inch up the block, cameras at the ready.

We creep around the corner just as a thirty-something man opens his front door to pick up his morning paper.

And then we pounce. POUNCE, I say. Standing there in his robe our guy is handed a cardboard check for $3 million dollars. With his name on it. Let's call him Scott.

Full-on COMMOTION. His confused family comes running outside. Many happy pajama hugs.

And then… as we look at each other it dawns…

"It's the guy in line in front of us at the deli! Wow, serendipity! The guy joking about winning! It's him! Why didn't he go straight home darn it?

He did say he was going out for the night, but hey, who knew it was him?"

Within minutes neighbors appear from every direction. Some of them look pissed.

And so it begins.

The Prize Patrol guy asks Scott, for the cameras, of course, "What will you do with the money?"

Scott immediately answers that his three children can now go to college.

(I love him for this. Love him).


The Patrol guy wants soundbites, and they ask Scott to call his boss and quit. He calls and says he isn't coming in today, but to come on over if he wants.

They ask Scott to call his mom and dad and tell them. They are shocked and excited. And on their way.

Word spreads. Within 10 minutes a happy crowd is gathering.

Or is it? Scott's neighbor says with a half-hearted chuckle, "Well I guess I don't have to help you paint your house anymore, huh?"

Scott's sister arrives to say, "Oh, we can all take a family vacation to Tahiti on you! When can we leave?"

Scott's best friend says, "I'm happy for you, dude. You know I need a new truck, right?"

In front of our very eyes, GREED is gathering. In less than 15 minutes the winner's life has changed. Scott will be expected to pick up the check for the rest of his life.

In the next two weeks Scott will get hundreds of letters and phone calls from perfect strangers asking for help. Sob stories one and all. They will slow, but never stop.

Scott's win will be how he is remembered. Or so it feels to him.

**He is famous now and it just might suck.**

## FOOTNOTE:

People who study lottery winners say it does. They recommend not telling anyone if at all possible. Before your friends and neighbors find out about your win move to a new town. Yes, it's that bad. This kind of fame almost always sucks. The money's nice but that's about it.

Years later, shooting the documentary ONE NATION UNDER STRESS, hosted by Merlin Olsen, I decide to include an unlikely self-help group for lottery winners who meet monthly on Staten Island.

There are ten people, all of whom have won, all of whom have lives that have changed in ways they hate.

Who can they trust anymore?

Are people just sucking up to them for money?

Why oh why do they ALWAYS have to pick up the check?

Why do people think they are so rich? After taxes it isn't nearly as much as people think.

Worst of all, they aren't recognized for their own achievements in life anymore, just for buying the damn ticket.

Today's meeting is a motley crew. Long Island housewives, a Russian Orthodox rabbi (whose congregation somehow now distrusts him), two social workers from Manhattan who bought the ticket together, a bus driver, a stockbroker, and a teacher. Under any other circumstances these folks are not likely to hang out. (I love this part of the story.)

These Sunday night meetings are potluck. Tonight, it's bagels, lasagna, and tortillas. Drinking cheap wine, they share their latest miseries of unwanted fame, of greed, the loss of so many friends, and more. Fresh stories every month.

It's a safe place to be with people who understand. And still, two people talked about how they now play the lottery incessantly. "Hey, I won once, I'm special, I can win again." "I won $20 bucks this week!"

Not easy being us they say. Not easy at all. Thank goodness we have each other.

## BOTTOM LINE:

**If at all possible be rich and anonymous. Rich and famous sucks, no matter how it happens.**

**Be careful what you wish for.**

# ME AND MRS. BARTLETT

Mrs. Bartlett was rich, but not famous. Except in certain circles, of course. Such an easier life, don't you think? Her first husband was Eli Lilly, president and board chair of Eli Lilly, the pharmaceutical company founded by his grandfather.

**In 1931 Evelyn married Frederic Clay Bartlett**

According to newspaper reports, "Evelyn Bartlett was the third wife of professional artist and art collector Frederic Clay Bartlett.

"Frederic Clay Bartlett, a painter and museum trustee in 1926 gave the Art Institute of Chicago an extraordinary collection of early modern masterpieces, including Georges Seurat's finest painting, "A Sunday on La Grande Jatte---1884."

Frederic and Evelyn endowed a room in the museum in honor of Helen Birch Bartlett, Frederic's second wife. She and Frederic had collected the paintings together. It was the first room devoted to modern art in any American museum, however reluctantly it was accepted. The endowment helped.

Frederic was the love of Evelyn's life and together they made their home in Fort Lauderdale, Bonnet House, into a whimsical masterpiece.

I met Mrs. Bartlett when she was 95.

Dillon Ripley, the head of the Smithsonian Museum, hired me to interview Evelyn at Bonnet House while she was still healthy. At her age it seemed prudent.

When she died her winter home would become a museum.

The shoot was a fun and easy getaway, I thought. I had no idea Mrs. Bartlett would change my life.

First there was the house. Bonnet House is 35 private, lush acres built between the ocean and the Intracoastal Waterway. It is constructed of exposed concrete blocks, painted in bright colors, and decorated with endless imagination. It took my breath away.

It is impossible to be pretentious in this house. It is spectacular. Just spectacular.

I've always had a quirky visual sense, and this was the house of my dreams. It was my taste writ large and in color.

Mrs. Bartlett and I immediately liked each other. This was 1983 and everybody was wearing patterned hose. The minute we met, Mrs. Bartlett took one look at mine and sent her butler out for some. By dinner in the courtyard, she was wearing her own, cut off above the knee and rolled down for comfort. Yep, we liked each other.

Every room was filled with color and pattern. Frederic had studied in Europe with Whistler among others. He was a talented painter whose work graced Bonnet House. After their marriage, Evelyn took up painting and together, they filled the walls.

Frederic and Evelyn's paintings fill the walls

Dozens of Brazilian squirrel monkeys rule the courtyard

Wild animals roam the halls and the home.

Exotic columns, cut in half, adorn the doorways.

This is a remarkable home. Not an ounce of pretension. Saturated colors. I went home to DC immediately and painted our walls Mrs. Bartlett Yellow and Mrs. Bartlett Blue. We've had these colors in every home we have lived in since.

**The house we live in now**

Each morning at Bonnet House, Mrs. Bartlett called me into the pantry while she carefully chose her china for the day's many occasions. Breakfast, lunch, tea in the orchid house (over 2,000 orchids), cocktails in the shell room, dinner in the courtyard. She approved the chef's menu but personally picked the china and silver. It was mix and match and different every meal. Including fingerbowls.

I screwed those up. Silly me, thinking they were for using. Dillon threw me such a look when I dipped my fingers in at lunch. "Oh Phyllis, don't you know anything?" I didn't and I still don't. Can somebody explain please?

Oh, and our breakfast eggs were flown in from her farm in Massachusetts. Yes, they were.

Old money indeed.

As we got to know each other in the pantry each morning, Mrs. Bartlett would tell me things:

"Frank (Lloyd Wright) loved Bonnet House, thought it was very clever. Not a happy man I don't think."

"I divorced Eli in 1927. It just wasn't done in those days. But he was boring."

"Don't be boring Phyllis. So many of the rich people I know are boring. Art, my monkeys, and my gardens keep me happy. Now help me make my rum punch."

Mrs. Bartlett changed me. Because of her, in just a few days I saw the world differently. She reinforced my love of whimsy. And humor. "A house has to laugh at itself," she said.

Mrs. Bartlett taught me how to be wealthy. Not that I'll ever need it, but now I know.

She taught me that nothing has to match. In fact, unmatched is much more fun.

Mrs. Bartlett taught me to embrace surprise. If I love it, I'll find a spot. But be picky too. Let go of your darlings. Let the room breathe.

Oh, and I learned to love her famous rum punch. She wouldn't share her recipe, though. Not with me anyway.

After the shoot, the two of us stayed in touch. Mrs. Bartlett would send me presents from Tiffany's at Christmas. Years later she invited me to her 100th birthday party, held at her farm in Beverly, Massachusetts.

One hundred people at round tables of eight in her garden. Oh, I was honored. I sat next to an old friend of hers, a man who'd spent most of his life exploring in Africa.

Mrs. Bartlett arrived at her party in grand style, sitting in an open carriage pulled by two horses and driven by Dillon Ripley wearing his top hat. An organ grinder and his monkey led the way, followed by strolling Romanian gypsies and bagpipes. It was triumphant.

One other thing Mrs. Bartlett taught me that I'm only now beginning to fully understand is her rule about sharing aches and pains. She invited friends on her yacht to travel with her each year and had no patience for such talk. Fined you ten bucks if you so much as mentioned one. A friend calls it an organ recital, and it's forbidden at my house, too. So boring.

Nine years after her party, Mrs. Bartlett died on July 1st, 1997. Two months before her 110th birthday. Fourteen years after we met. Never once complaining to a friend.

## EVELYN BARTLETT, 109, ARTS PATRON

**By Alan G. Artner and Tribune Art Critic**
**Chicago Tribune July 02, 1997**

Evelyn Fortune Bartlett, one of the last great links to the Gilded Age of cultural life in Chicago, died Tuesday in her home in Beverly, Mass. The arts patron and painter was 109.

I loved this woman, and I think she loved me.

Oh, how lucky I was to have her in my life.

**So much better than fame.**

# ME AND THE EARL OF NORTHUMBERLAND
## PART ONE
### 1979

My favorite Harry Percy story is our dinner out at a Capitol Hill dive called The Tune Inn. For once he was paying. Being English royalty didn't make you generous.

"Hey, Earl, this credit card won't work," barks the waitress. "You signed your name Harry. It says right on the card your name is Earl, Earl Percy."

The look on Harry's face....

He always wore an ascot. His skin was translucent. His accent public school. Queen Elizabeth was his godmother. He was named after Harry Percy, the Hotspur of Shakespeare.

None of this made Harry happy. He was, in fact, one of the saddest people I've ever known.

He showed up at our Capitol Hill row house, towed by one of the neighbors. One of ten people squeezed into our tiny dining room for Sunday brunch. Cheap champagne and bagels and hours of hooting laughter. Oh, it was fun! For the next year and a half, Harry came to brunch often but never quite got the hang of it. People would ask me who that boring guy with the ascot was.

Harry's Dad, The Duke of Northumberland

His father the Duke had pulled a favor from Dillon Ripley, the head of the Smithsonian. "Harry isn't right," the Duke said. "He is depressed, he needs help." But help, the Duke felt, was impossible in England. Finding a shrink to treat the Earl of Northumberland... well, it just wasn't done. Of course, shrink is not the word he used.

The Duchess suggested Harry be sent for treatment in DC. Perhaps he could live with the Ripleys and come home when he was better. Dillon and his wife took one look at sad sack Harry and foisted him off on an underling, my neighbor, Ralph Rinzler. And so, Harry moved in, but he still needed a shrink. That is where I came in. Could I introduce Harry to mine? Sure. Bring him to brunch.

It seems this tale of Harry and me is doomed to be interrupted by back stories. Which is usually a bummer, but in this case is the real reason Harry's story is interesting.

I'll try to keep it short, but this is an old family so don't expect a lot.

As I soon learned, Harry was not like you or me. So, why did the Duke call Dillon? Family connections of course. James Smithson was the illegitimate son of the first Duke of Northumberland, Hugh Percy. His father never acknowledged James. Even so, Smithson prospered, making a bundle. When he died in 1829, the Percys will tell you, Smithson left all his money to the one place his father hated more than any other—that upstart America. The scientific institution he designated in his will was named after him. Oh, sweet irony.

Here's a painting of James Smithson, c.1786. You can see it in the National Portrait Gallery of the Smithsonian.

150 years after Smithson's bequest, the Percys and the Smithsonian gingerly made up. On a visit to England, Ripley's oozing overtook old grudges. The Duke agreed to loan the Smithsonian a painting or two, Ripley made a fuss, and all was once again well. Not once again, I guess. Finally. It was a major relief for all concerned.

Harry spent almost a year in DC, untangling his emotional life. We all thought he was starting to perk up when his mom yanked him home. I thought it was because she didn't really like the new Harry. Pretty common, I think.

**1981**

Now Harry is back in London and I'm in DC but coming his way shortly to be a field producer/director/writer for a silly Hollywood show called YOU ASKED FOR IT, starring Rich Little. It was temporary, as all television jobs are temporary. Adventures await.

I'll be traveling through Europe and Africa and based in London. I called Harry. Possible to stay with you?

Of course, you can stay.

"Syon House is near the airport," Harry says. "Very convenient, don't you think?"

"Sounds great, Harry. Sure you have room?" "Not a problem," says he. "My parents spend most of their time in Northumberland and there's plenty of room. You have to walk down the hall to the bathroom though." "Too bad we don't have the house downtown anymore," he says. "That would have been perfect for you, right on Trafalgar Square.

But they tore it down to build Charing Cross." As if I had just missed it.

"Oh, what a shame," say I. "Syon will be fun, Harry. I like hanging out with you."

A few weeks later I disembark from the Concorde at Heathrow (Hollywood perc) and taxi to Syon House, stepping further into Harry's world.

**I had no idea what a world it was. None.**

# WORDS TO LIVE BY

Row, row, row your boat
Gently down the stream
Merrily, merrily, merrily, merrily
Life is but a dream.

# MORE OF ME AND EARL PERCY
## PART TWO

Decades later, this "downtown" house of Harry's comes up in a novel I'm reading. I click my way to **Northumberland House** on the Strand. Oh my.

As you might recall, this is the house Harry said would be so convenient for my time in London but "they tore it down to build Charing Cross." Seems that was in 1875. There had been a fire and the city needed the land to build the Charing Cross Underground. Alrighty then, Harry.

The "house" was built in 1605 for the Duke of Northampton and bought by the Percys in the 1640s for fifteen thousand pounds. Even then, it seems a bargain for the largest private home in London.

Yep, room for me. And so convenient, just like Harry said.

Here's the thing, Harry wasn't bragging, just being the Earl of Northumberland.

A few years earlier, shortly after we met back in DC, Harry casually explained to me that if the British hadn't lost the Battle of Hastings in 1066, his father would now be king.

It wasn't easy being Harry. Not at all. The world that was seemed to be over and his place in the world that is now was a confusing place for him. And a full-time job.

Here are two more Percy family homes. The main ones, I mean.

The biggest deal is Alnwick Castle, the family seat, in Northumberland:

*"Alnwick Castle is the second largest inhabited castle in England, and has been the ancestral seat of the Percys, Earls and Dukes of Northumberland since 1309."*

That's over 700 years of history. If you go to the movies at all you've probably seen Alnwick Castle without knowing it.

A gaggle of Harry Potter movies were filmed here and the movie ELIZABETH, starring Cate Blanchett.

Syon House can brag about some cool movies, too: EMMA, with Gwyneth Paltrow, THE MADNESS OF KING GEORGE, and my personal favorite, THE AVENGERS. Oh, and scenes from BRIDGERTON were filmed here.

*Syon House and its 200 acres is the London home of the Duke of Northumberland. It's on the north bank of the Thames and 8 miles from London.*

Now back to me and Harry:

When Harry came home from DC, he had lots of places to live, he said. "We Percys are the second largest landowners in England, right after the Queen. We have estates all over the place. But Syon House is close to London and my parents spend most of their time at Alnwick. I'm 26 and want my own space."

And so, as I mentioned earlier, I flew to Heathrow on the Concorde, courtesy of Hollywood. As instructed, I asked the taxi driver to take me to Syon House. He didn't believe me—balked at going in the gates, sure we were intruders. I bounced up the front steps and banged on the massive door. No answer.

It was dark, about 10:30 at night. The driver wanted the hell out of there, convinced we were about to be arrested. He started dumping my luggage in the driveway while I honked his horn. Servants eventually appeared, escorted me to bed, brought a hot brick swathed in needlepoint to warm my toes and there I was, at Harry's house.

In the morning. Harry told me I'd been sleeping in the Princess Victoria bedroom. On her very bed. With its original mattress, too. "Actually," he explained, "it has three mattresses—a bottom one of straw, the second of horsehair, and the top layer is filled with goose feathers." It seems the Princess and her mom spent a lot of time at Syon because the third Duchess of Northumberland was the royal governess.

Here's a picture of my bedroom:

## It's 1981, and my overseas television adventures begin...

# MICHAEL WARD AROUND THE WORLD
## SUCH A GOOD TRAVELER

Oh, I missed him. I still can't believe we managed it. Ms. I'm-So-Liberated is off on another adventure. Not quite sure when I'll be back, oh-love-of-my-life. I'll be in touch.

Most of the years of my many travels, Michael was hard at work saving the planet. Working as Counsel for the Energy and Power Subcommittee on Capitol Hill. Congressman John Dingell of Detroit was the legendary head of the committee. It was Michael's dream job. He did important things while I had adventures. So far, he is refusing to write them down. Damn him.

I had been traveling in and out of London for months, working for Hollywood wherever I was sent—lately it'd been hopping around small countries in Europe, scarfing up stories.

Michael and I would talk at least once a week. More! Not really, but we tried. This was before cell phones. As soon as they were available we rejoiced, of course, but I was often in places that didn't have service.

But we tried to stay in touch. One beautiful day my intrepid crew and I were in a field outside of Dublin. For a reason that now escapes me we were recording an Irish tenor singing that ultimate ballad,

I started crying for my missing Irishman. Sobbing really. I pulled out the picture of Michael I carried with me and held it up for us both to listen together. It helped a little.

# DANNY BOY

*O Danny boy, the pipes, the pipes are calling*

*From glen to glen and down the mountainside*

*The summer's gone and all the roses falling*

*'Tis you, 'tis you must go and I must bide*

*But come ye back when summer's in the meadow*

*Or all the valley's hushed and white with snow*

*'Tis I'll be here in sunshine or in shadow*

*O Danny boy, O Danny boy, I love you so*

The next day he went to explore the church
mummies with me.

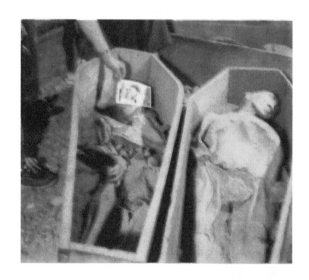

And soon my wonderful crew blew up my small picture to clipboard size. **Michael Ward Around the World** was born. We had adventures together. For decades.

When Michael visited me in London a few months later, he posed.

When asked to hold Michael's picture, not one person ever said no.

It was great.

Here are just a few pictures of his many, many travels.

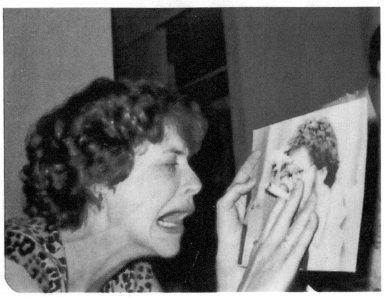

## Oh I missed him so!

Clearly, Michael and I made the right decision to not have children. They would have died of neglect. There is a famous story about a 60 Minutes producer who was stuck overseas longer than she expected and came home to her dead cat. The person who was feeding him had bailed. It swept around our industry as a cautionary tale. But what was there to do about it really?

Amazingly, or maybe it wasn't, our marriage was more than fine. It was flourishing. Somehow we stumbled into a relationship that is fun everyday.

With the wisdom of a great therapist, we had given up our hippie ways of "nobody owns anybody" for this new idea of "mutual ownership".

Stay with me now, 'cause this is central to understanding me.

## THE WORLD ACCORDING TO PHYLLIS:

In the 60s, birth control liberated women. Sex was fun. And if you did it right, safe.

We feminists believed that women had been owned for millenium but now nobody owned anybody. Lesley Gore's hit, YOU DON'T OWN ME, was just one of our feminist anthems. Whoohoo.

Even if you weren't promiscuous you could be. We finally had total agency over our bodies and ourselves.

But it turns out that wasn't a safe place. At least not for me. For Michael and me. Us.

I grew up in a family that wasn't a safe place. Didn't know what one felt like. When Michael and I married our unspoken contract was that we were together for as long as we wanted to be. We were in love and hanging out.

What my wonderful therapist taught us was the joy of MUTUAL OWNERSHIP. The knowledge that I own you and you own me. No need to swallow anything or hold back when we were angry. None of this slow burn or last straw stuff for us.

Wow, what a change. Think about this for a minute. This mutual ownership deal creates a totally safe place. I'm always the first to know if there's a problem. If you don't speak up, I know we are cool. If I sense a problem, I call you on it immediately. YOU OWN ME and I OWN YOU and we don't swallow our feelings. What a liberating idea. It struck me as anti-feminist at first. But it's the exact opposite. Total equality. Took awhile to get it but when we did we both realized we were both in a safe place for the first time in our lives.

It allowed both of us to go off on our burgeoning career adventures, wherever they might take us, without worrying about the strength of our relationship.

Like all marriages, mutual ownership doesn't mean we won't break up. But in ours, there will be no unspoken festering. We both know that if there is a problem one of us will flag it immediately.

One or the other of us have called in our ownership rights dozens of times over the course of 52 years. But there have been no secrets.

What a difference it's made in our lives.

We are both free to trust each other, to wallow in each other, to just have fun together. In our marriage it's essential.

After years of separate travels, we mutually decided we wouldn't be apart physically for more than 3 months. Not that it happened often, mind you, but that was what worked for us. No more crying in the fields.

```
    WJA196(1126)(1-013233A280)PD  10/07/81  1126
ICS IPMWGWC WSH                              1981 OCT -7  PM 12: 39
 07091 10-07 1216P EDT
ICS IPMWJ08
1-1043330G280 10/07/81
ICS IPMIIHA IISS
   IISS F M RCA 07 1042
PMS WASHINGTON DC
 WUB5353 LZB8096   QAG8707 FFU051900 GBTT244
URIX CO URTL 020
QUEENELIZABETH2 MARISAT 20/19 07 1134
MICHAEL WARD
20 8THST.SE
WASHINGTON/DC
SHIP DELAYED ARRIVE NEWYORK FRIDAY AM SEE YOU EARLY EVENING CANT WAIT
LOVE PHYLLIS
```

Michael's back from his travels now.
Now he sits in my office window, quietly
remembering the good times.

## I'm so lucky

# PRODUCER LESSONS
# LEARNING TO BE NIMBLE
## Or what to do when your plan goes to shit.

We arrive in plenty of time. Excited to be here. We've come all the way from London to Langata, Kenya to film the giraffes.

The Manor House is a giraffe sanctuary owned by Jock and Betty Leslie-Melville. He's the Earl of Leven's grandson, Betty is his American wife. They bought the dilapidated home and are restoring it as a sanctuary for the endangered Rothschild giraffes.

In 2023, it's now a famous hotel called Giraffe Manor, with prices starting at $875 per night per person. When we arrive back in 1981, only Betty is there to greet us. Jock is in London. She welcomes us warmly and shows us where to set up. We are here to shoot the giraffes, of course.

Every day, in the late afternoon, five or six giraffes come right up to the manor, sticking their long necks through second story windows and first floor door to say hello and grab a carrot.

How cool is this?

But today no giraffes. None. "How strange," says Betty. "How very strange."

We sit in the parlor with our camera gear at our feet and wait. And wait.

Betty makes tea. The servants are off, and she has no idea how it's done. I help. We are both pitiful at something as simple as making tea, the guys are laughing at us.

Now the sun is starting to go down. STILL no giraffes. What to do?

We are here and we are leaving for the bush tomorrow.

Arrggghhhh. I am trying not to panic. This is an important story to my Hollywood bosses; they plan to use some of the footage in the series open each night. Tick tock. Still no giraffes.

The only thing I can see on the horizon are warthogs.

Okayyyyyy, says Ms. Directorwoman.

Warthogs it is.

Not what Hollywood wants, but hey. This is what Hollywood gets.

I'm proud of myself for my quick thinking. Don't panic, Phyllis. Calm.

Except warthogs are feisty. Dangerous, even. Those tusks can hurt.

Crew not happy at all.

**AND THEN.... HERE THEY COME...**

At the very last minute. And there is just enough light to shoot. We hustle. We all know exactly what we need to do, and we do it.

Amazing ourselves.

We end our day with two stories, not just one.

When the sun goes down, we have a civilized tea, with bourbon. My heart eventually stops racing. That day I learned one of the most important lessons of my television life:

Be prepared. Overprepared, actually. Only when I know what I want to accomplish backwards and forwards, only then can I regroup when my plan disintegrates.

Only then do I relax enough to look around me calmly and see what else might work. (Sometimes calmer than others, mind you.) Only because of all my Deep Preparation can I take advantage of serendipity when things run amuck. That day in Kenya with the giraffes I learned to never panic. My new mantra became: "Hey it's only TV."

It turns out that some of the very best things happen when my plan goes to shit.

## True in life too.

# WORDS TO LIVE BY:
# TRY SOFTER

"Why does everyone always tell you to try harder?"
says Lily Tomlin.

I'm trying as hard as I can. Trying softer is a better
bet.

I heard Lily say this in a standup routine long, long
ago and it is the most useful piece of advice I've ever
received.

Just relax, Phyllis. Breathe, woman. Look around
you.

## TRY SOFTER.

Give it a shot. I use it every day.

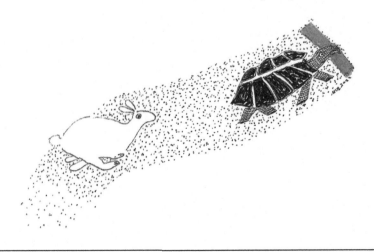

# ME AND EDVARD MUNCH
## 1979

"Your problem," says Linda, "is you have a choice."
We're sitting at an outdoor cafe having lunch and
talking about babies.

I'm 31, if I want babies, it's time to get on with it.
Linda is 52 and has three grown kids. "When I got
married babies just happened," she continued, "but
now there's the pill—you get to choose. Poor you."
Linda was absolutely right. We thought we were
liberated but damn.

Michael and I had been trying to decide for years
now. I hate that word try. You either decide or you
don't. It all seemed so complicated—I had one baby
foot in a television career and the learning curve was
all consuming. We talked about it often with no
results. "Do you want kids?" I'd ask. "Do you?" he'd
answer. One spring morning I went to see the
**Edvard Munch** exhibit at the National Gallery of
Art. It was a blockbuster show of 240 paintings.

I knew Munch from THE SCREAM and not much else.

"For several years I was almost mad..." Munch wrote, "You know my picture, The Scream? I was stretched to the limit—nature was screaming in my blood... After that I gave up hope ever of being able to love again."

I learned Munch was hospitalized for a nervous breakdown in 1908 and lived what could only be described as a miserable life. The exhibition notes were chilling.

For the next two mesmerized hours, I went through the exhibit twice.

I'd never seen anything like it. This man was brutally honest. The show was in chronological order and each self-portrait showed an increasingly depressed man. I knew this because I had worked at a psychiatric hospital and was taught the physical signs of clinical depression. A depressed person's face has a furrowed brow and lips that turn down at the corners.

Every one of Munch's self-portraits were textbook illustrations. Decade by decade, you could see his depression grow worse. I can't imagine Munch knew what he was painting—what did he know about the symptoms of clinical depression? He just looked in the mirror and painted what he saw. Unflinchingly.

The man had every opportunity to cheat a little, make himself look less haunted, but he didn't. It was remarkable.

Had I ever been that brutally honest with myself? I slunk to a bench on the mall, sat in the sunshine and decided to give it a try. Okay, babies. What to do about babies? Let's think it through.

I had just finished reading a biography about one of my heroes, the groundbreaking anthropologist Margaret Mead, and was bummed to find out she was a terrible mother and a lousy wife. (Mead scholars may say I got it all wrong, but this is how it seemed to me.) Even worse, her ground-breaking fieldwork was now being disputed. It was clear she did a less than perfect job at all three.

Hmmm... did I know anyone who was doing better? I knew women who were terrific mothers, I knew women who had great marriages, and I knew women who had major careers. But all three? No, I didn't. I could think of a handful that were successful at two out of three.

Maybe it's different now, but in 1979 we who considered ourselves liberated were on a tear. Wearing power suits with polyester bows and lugging briefcases, each of us was determined to break the damn glass ceiling. I imagined it as the second highest floor of a skyscraper and filled with light from above, sort of like heaven. I never quite knew what we were supposed to use, our heads? An ax? In 1979, I was still in the television sub-basement and atingle to be working 70-hour weeks doing the scut work for men with big egos who felt threatened. (I know, you are thinking surely there were men with small egos, but don't forget this was broadcast television.)

Television is sort of a meritocracy, though, and so I was sent to Tahiti on a moment's notice to produce a story about plastic surgery. I called Michael and took off. No time to stash a baby, that's for sure.

Sitting here on my bench, once again endlessly mulling over my options, it dawned on me that I had been constant in my self-analysis, ruminating for years now on how to pull off marriage, motherhood, and a real career. But I hadn't been merciless.

I knew I was incredibly lucky to have a marriage with a capital M. Not a slam dunk by any means but so far, we were making it happen. Can't let that slip.

My television career was just taking off. I was consumed with moving up and was in hot pursuit of a career with a capital C. And I wasn't about to be a mother unless I could be a damn good one, much better than my own. Mother with a capitol M.

Just like that, it was totally obvious to me, all this time I'd been asking the wrong question. I was frozen because I assumed, like many of my friends, that I was expected to do all three equally well. But using my brand-new Munch mirror, well, I wasn't nearly up to it. I knew in my marrow I couldn't pull off all three roles with anything approaching joy. It was silly to even try. More than silly, stupid.

And so, I watched tourists stroll by while I sat in the sunshine and picked two out of three. Clearly and irrevocably. It was just that easy. In my life, at least, babies were out of the question.

## Thanks, Edvard.

# NEARNESS TO GREATNESS
# OPRAH

Success is a slippery thing. Serendipity plays its part, of course. Always.

And we do, too. My motto has always been that if it's not scary, it's not worth doing. Kinda stupid, huh? And guarantees a life of stress.

I'm over that now. In 1983, I worked at WJZ in Baltimore down the hall from Oprah Winfrey. I was the documentary producer and Oprah co-hosted a local talk show, PEOPLE ARE TALKING. My good friend and former intern, Debbie DiMaio, was hired as a producer at WLS-TV in Chicago—a much bigger pond than Baltimore. Debbie had just left PEOPLE ARE TALKING and was excited about her new job. The station manager saw Oprah on Debbie's sample reel and offered Oprah a job as host of their morning show, AM CHICAGO.

One night, I got a phone call at home from Oprah.

I was known for being supportive. And frank.

Oprah said a (higher up in station management who
will remain nameless) had just taken her to dinner.

Her voice cracked through the phone as she said this
person told her:

"Oprah, you're a fat, black girl who's a big fish in a
small pond. If you go to Chicago, you will fail."

HUH? Say that again? "I'm a fat, black girl who's a
big fish in a small pond. If I take the job, I'll fail."

Oh shut up and take the job, woman.

And take it she did.

I'm not saying our conversation made the difference.
Surely by morning Oprah had come to her senses.
And I'm sure every one of her friends said the same
thing I did. At best, I'm a footnote in her life.

But what if she had listened? Only Oprah knows
how close she came to passing it by.

**I've always told this story as being a footnote
in Oprah's autobiography. Wonder if she'd
mention it.**

**Nearness to greatness indeed.**

# SEIZE YOUR POWER

There are moments in everyone's life when you surprise yourself.

Doing something you didn't expect to do, didn't really think you could do. In my life these have always been moments of great change. When I talk to my friends about these moments, the stories are dramatic. This is one of mine.

I am a field producer at a local station churning out two 7-minute stories a week. Find them, shoot them, write them, supervise the edit. Repeat. These are light and bright stories most of the time, but I also do kids with cancer and people with agoraphobia.

It's a lot of work, especially if you include the find-them part.

This is my first paying job in television and it's an exhilarating grind. There are two of us. The second story producer has recently been recruited from out of town.

We struggle to keep up. One day, the talk show (with offices on the same floor) comes to me to ask me if I'd be interested in producing their show. How flattering. But not really, I love the field, talking to people in their natural habitat.

That very same day I find out that my fellow producer is making $20,000 more than I am, even though I've been there longer. Huh?

This will not stand, says Ms. Feminist.

I march up the stairs to the appropriate boss's office demanding a hearing.


Me: First of all, Mr. Pooh-bah, I'm not interested in the talk show job, but thanks for the offer. I'm very surprised it didn't come with a raise. And speaking of raises, it has come to my attention that my fellow story producer is making $20,000 more than I am. What's up with that?

Him: Well, Phyllis, he's a man.

Me: A man? Really? You've heard of this new thing going around called equal pay for equal work, right?

Him: Yes, but he's a man.

Me: Are your ears clogged?

Him: But, but...

Me: And you know I'm a better producer.

Him: Yes, but...but...

Me: Equal pay for equal work.

Him: I can't do any better, Phyllis

Me: You can't do any better? I'm going downstairs to go think about this. I'll give you my answer in an hour, I say, as I stomp out.

I sit in my office with my red cowboy boots up on my desk, smoking a Macanudo cigar, puffing very slowly. I call Michael. He agrees. "Quit. Equal pay for equal work. We'll figure it out." Now mind you, it has taken me years to get into this business. But still.

When the cigar is just a stub I go back up to the pooh-bah's office.

Me: I quit. You have my two-week notice.

Him: What would it take to make you stay?

Me: I think I was pretty clear. Equal pay for equal work.

Long pause.

Him: You've got it, you cunt, he says storming out of his office and slamming the door.

Seizing your power indeed. It felt
wonderful.

But don't EVER call me a cunt. EVER.

# WHEN EVERY SECOND COUNTS

It's 1987. Cameraman Gino, soundman Jeff, associate producer Kandy, and I are shooting CRITICAL MINUTES, a documentary about the newly emerging concept of Trauma Care. The Golden Hour, it is called.

Dr. R. Adams Cowley is the trauma surgeon promoting this idea. Cowley's opinion was "There is a golden hour between life and death. If you are critically injured, you have less than 60 minutes to survive. You might not die right then; it may be three days or two weeks later — but something has happened in your body that is irreparable."

We have spent many nights at the University of Maryland Shock Trauma Center watching Dr. Crowley and his team in action.

And now here we are in Winnemucca, Nevada, precisely because it is sooooo isolated. Humboldt County, of which Winnemucca is the county seat, is 9,658 square miles with a population of around 16,000.

That works out to 1.7 people per square mile. More sheep than people. Lots of tumbleweed. Not a Golden Hour kind of place. What happens, we want to know, if you need urgent medical help here?

The mayor meets us at the diner to welcome us to town.

He's wearing blue jeans and a bright red baseball hat that says WhattheFucksaWinnemucca? Really, that's what it says.

Think I'm gonna like it here.

The mayor takes us to meet the town doctor, who tells us, yes, there are sometimes very bad accidents. A Basque shepherd, tending his sheep, poked his eye out on a wire fence last week. Lives over 70 miles away, up in the mountains. His nearest neighbor is 22 miles east. In a different area code.

By the time the shepherd found a ride to town, says the doctor, it was too late to save his eye.

He takes us on a tour of town, past what he calls the local "cat house," where he checks the workers bimonthly for sexually transmitted diseases, as required by law. The women are friendly, telling us that their main customers are those Basque farmers who come into town twice a year to sell their sheep.

As we continue our town tour, the doc tells me, "Once a year the girls invite the Basque wives to tea and offer up new and slightly used lacy underwear," to the oh-so-modest and grateful shepherds' wives.

Did I mention I think I'm gonna like it here?
The doctor sends us off to meet the ambulance driver. He's the gentleman on the right.

We've been told he's the best source for exactly what happens to you if you have a life-threatening injury in Humboldt County.

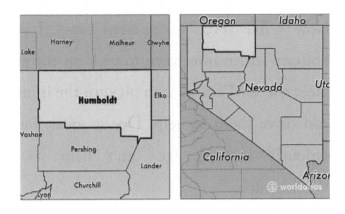

## HUMBOLT COUNTY NEVADA

Q: What happens if you have a bad accident in Humboldt County?

A: "So," the friendly ambulance driver explains, "first, someone has to find you. If you have an accident out here at night, that might take a while. Did they tell you it's over 9,500 square miles? Not a lot of people on these roads. Day or night, really. Now once they find you, they find a phone and call it in."

(NOTE: I hate to admit this, but we shot this doc before cell phones. Geez I'm old. Not that many of these areas, even today, are likely to have coverage.)

Now I live seven miles from town. I put on my uniform, drive into town to pick up the ambulance, meet the EMT and then pick up the injured person and drive them to help. Doc is great, but if you're seriously injured, we can't help you here in Winnemucca."

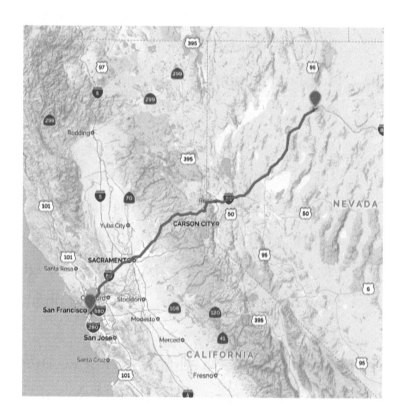

"So we drive you in the ambulance to the nearest Trauma Center at San Francisco General. (NOTE: 383 miles away) It's about a five-and-a-half-hour drive to San Francisco General, with lights flashing; I've done it in four-and-a-half. It's too far for a helicopter, but sometimes they fly to meet us part way, depends on how bad off you are."

Q: "So best case?" I ask.

A: "So best case," he answers, "if all goes well, we can get you to a trauma center in five or six hours. If everything breaks your way. It's tough."

Q: "As you know, doctors now know how crucial the Golden Hour is to saving lives. Every minute counts. You are on the front lines. What do you think can be done in a place like Humboldt County to save lives?"

A: "Well, see my uniform?" he says without hesitation as he opens his jacket and points to his shirt. "My wife replaced all my buttons with Velcro. Saves me time when they call me to go pick up the ambulance.

When every minute counts indeed.

This has always been one of my favorite TV stories. The optimism of this ambulance driver in face of what seemed like overwhelming odds. His determination to do his part.

**Some days it feels like all we can do is get out the Velcro.**

# EQUAL

# MY ADVENTURES IN JAPAN

## PART ONE

Equal is a tricky, tricky concept.

Trickier than truth, if you ask me. It's true. Or is it?

We Americans brag about our country's belief in equality constantly. Equal rights, equal opportunity. Damn it, let's march. I don't care what the Constitution says, the average American doesn't believe for a minute that we are all created equal. From kindergarten on, some of us do better than others and all of us know exactly who that is. Raise your hand please, says the teacher, all of your contributions are of equal value. But that's horse poop and we know it. Even before we stop saying poop, we know it.

But some cultures are much better than we are in the day-to-day practice of equality. I learned that in Japan.

I was directing a series for PBS called FACES OF JAPAN. The Japanese had already shot this series once themselves, but PBS rejected it as too Japanese for an American audience. This time the Japanese were putting two Americans on every crew—a director (me) and a cameraman (Kevin). There would be a Japanese producer, soundman, gaffer, and translator. Dick Cavett would show up for a week of weaving the stories together. This time it would work. Together we would bring Japan to America. Hardly.

**LESSON ONE:** Americans are direct, Japanese are unequivocally not. Meeting with our new Japanese bosses was an all-day affair and my initiation into never, ever, ever saying what you mean. It took me forever to figure out that in Japan yes, yes, yes often means no, no, no. At seven or eight hours at a stretch, getting to a real yes was unequivocally exhausting. (And I'm not sure these meetings took so long because I was dense. I sort of think that is the way it's done. Later, it was extremely useful training for dealing with American network executives, but at the time, I just didn't get it.)

The closest I'd come to actually understanding this core Japanese belief—that everyone's contribution is of equal value—was my stint at a psychiatric hospital in Washington, DC. I was the director of education which somehow included working with patients. It had been my bright idea to send video cameras home on weekend passes with patients. They were to return with footage of life at home, giving the shrinks insight into home dynamics—something that is always important to shrinks. When our trial patient returned with close-ups of every knife in the house, well let's just say the experiment was abandoned as potentially risky. And admissible in court. And so, it was decided that each unit would create a welcome video—sort of a "day in the life of" for new patients, to get them in the swing more quickly. This was decades before cell phone videos, not to mention decades before cell phones, so this little assignment was a major production. Lights, camera, tripods, microphones, monitors, mixers, and miles of cable to hook it all together. I assigned each person on the unit a job according to my evaluation of their skills.

As you can imagine it was a motley crew, what with folks being in various stages of psychosis.

But something remarkable happened. It was clear to every single one of us that each of us had to do our part to make this work. We couldn't make this movie without the cooperation of even the mute man in the corner. It was his job to flip the switch for the camera lights—on and off as needed. The fact that he hadn't said a word in the two weeks he had been on the unit didn't stop him from clicking away as directed. Making a movie wasn't like school. Here, each person's contribution really did matter.

And at that moment I learned what makes a great director. It was my job to motivate every single person who even peripherally touched my films to do their best. This wasn't like grade school, any of them—even the lowliest, could fuck it up. None of them could be ignored or looked down upon. Each of us was crucial to the final product.

This insight was the key to my (modest) success. Later, every time I was asked to speak at some seminar or another about the secrets of good producing and directing, I would always tell this story.

Understanding that everyone's contribution is of equal importance is the essence of good filmmaking. That and always feed your crew.

How very Japanese, huh?

I have dozens more examples from my time in Japan, but I'll spare you. Maybe somewhere Aiko is writing a snippet about his experiences with clueless Americans. I don't blame him. We both have gripes. Even though we both speak English, his facts aren't my facts. His equal isn't my equal.

## Tricky, tricky.

# TELEVISION WORDS TO LIVE BY:

## ENTERTAIN CHAOS

1. Isolate the problem. Don't put answers in your questions.
2. Don't limit yourself.
3. Try various viewpoints.
4. Be aware of stereotypes and preconceptions.
5. Watch out for saturation.
6. Use ALL your senses.
7. Watch out for cultural and environmental blocks (taboos, traditions).
8. Am I afraid of taking a risk? (Catastrophic expectations)
9. Creating is messy.
10. Generate, don't judge.
11. Relax and sleep on it.
12. Do I care enough but not too much?
13. Am I using the correct language?

Did she say Entertain Chaos?

# PRODUCER LESSONS

# WHAT I LEARNED ABOUT BOSSES

Leonard Stern was a very big time Hollywood producer, writer, and director. You will know from shows like Get Smart, McMillian and Wife, The Honeymooners and many, many more. I had the great privilege of interviewing Leonard once. He adopted me, becoming my friend until he died in 2011.

In 1991, Leonard and Diane Robinson published a book called A MARTIAN WOULDN'T SAY THAT: Urgent Memos TV Execs Wish They Hadn't Written.

Here are a few examples:

1. To Leonard Stern

Unfortunately, we are forced to put your program on hiatus.

It has elements of quality for which we can't find an audience.

2. To: The Producers

FROM: VP, Current Programming

RE: MY FAVORITE MARTIAN

Please change the dialogue on page 14. A Martian wouldn't say that.

3. To: The Producers

From: VP, Current Programming

RE: Fred Astaire Special

Too much dancing.

4. And my personal favorite. "Can we make the rabbi less Jewish?"

Ha! So how DID these folks get in charge? Like bosses everywhere, that's how. Here are a few favorites from my personal experience:

1. I was once told by an executive producer, "This documentary about the desert is *too brown*, please fix."

2. And..."We can't air this, it has too many black holes!" Huh? The half hour in question is a rough cut, a cut edited so that six executives in three different locations on this phone call can agree on the content. Until you guys do that, I have learned it is a total waste

of time and money to add pictures. After three long years of endless recuts, it finally occurred to me to send a cut without pictures, just soundbites. It became known in our office as the "radio cut".

One day on reviewing this show, the comment was "too many black holes." Spoken by a network intern who had been elevated to the phone call by his boss, as said boss was unavailable. Poor guy was desperate to contribute. Which is the wisdom I now offer to you—in television or not, for anyone with a boss.

**Keep reading.**

I am a new hire at a TV station as documentary producer. My new boss says he wants to get to know me. A few days before, I won a very big deal award for the station just as I left to come to work here. He sits me down to let us look at the winning doc together.

His head is inches from the screen, searching, searching. Very weird. It's an hour documentary. About 35 minutes into it he pokes his finger to stop the video.

"There, right there," he says. "It's a jumpcut."

"Where?"

"Right there," he says.

We rewind, rewatch, and find no jumpcut. My new boss insists we look again. Nope.

"Oh," he says, "well, we don't tolerate jumpcuts at this station. Be sure you don't have any."

"Yes sir!"

In that instant, I think I figured out what was really going on. Perhaps he was a little intimidated by my award. He wanted to be sure I knew he was the boss. He had important contributions to make. Always. All bosses feel this way. If we can't contribute, what good are we? So, from that day forward, I'd always leave my bosses something to fix.

1. "Oh, you found that jumpcut! You saved the show!" (See above)

2. "Yes, there is a typo on page 6 of the script. I'll fix it." (You DO know the script won't be seen on air, don't you?)

3. "You're right, that sponsor name in the credits IS spelled wrong. Thank goodness you caught it!"

At heart, these were good people who wanted to say something constructive or wanted to assert their power. Or sometimes both.

After they had pointed out my mistake the rest of their note were much easier. With large groups, I'd start by asking them all to answer a question for me to solve a problem for me before we got into the weeds.

Now please understand that many of my bosses had very constructive things to say.
But still. This was a major insight for me. It worked wonderfully for me for decades.

## I'm a bitch. This is true.

## Use it as you will.

## But don't ever call me a cunt.

# FACTOIDS I LOVE

## A pencil between your teeth can make you happier

**Another factoid TV research brought me
that I use every day**

"Put a pencil between your teeth in just the right way, and you'll feel happier—though you won't know why."

*Kelly McGonigal, a psychologist at Stanford University, reports:*

"This effect demonstrates **the "facial feedback" theory of emotion**—but you can think of it as "fake it till you make it." The idea is simple: your brain is constantly monitoring what's happening in your body. It analyzes things like muscle tension, posture, heart rate, breathing, and, yes, facial expressions, to judge how you are feeling.

Put yourself in a happier position, and you can boost your mood. The pencil trick works because it forces your face to mimic a genuine smile, recruiting just the muscles of the mouth, cheeks, and eyes that come to life when you are happy."

Just by putting a pencil in your mouth in this horizontal way, your lips automatically form the shape of a smile. And your body recognizes it. How cool is that?

And yes, I knew you'd ask, I no longer need the pencil. Can you see me faking a smile? It totally works.

## Aren't factoids great?

# MOST EMBARRASSING
# MOMENT OF MY LIFE

## THE EARL AND ME
## CONTINUED...PART THREE

## SYON HOUSE, LONDON SUMMER
## 1981

Very quickly Harry and I settled in. I traveled a lot
and kept a dank studio in Kensington, but I used
Syon as my base. A place to do laundry and recover.
The hot bricks always helped.

I sound cavalier, don't I? I wasn't. It took us a while to figure out how to talk to each other. One night at dinner, Harry's father went on about the Percy who fought in the Revolutionary War. That's pretty amazing, I thought, and then slowly realized he fought for the British.

Harry tried to cover my embarrassment, chiming in about the 9th Earl's youngest brother, George Percy, who was one of the original settlers of Jamestown in 1607. His father threw in Walker Percy, the southern novelist, but none of it made me feel better. I was soooo American, Harry was sooooo English. We dabbled in each other.

That summer the Duke and Duchess gave a party at Syon in honor of Charles and Di's upcoming wedding.

Charlton Heston came, and enough people to fill the Long Gallery—which you can see is very, very long. Harry told me he learned to ride his bike in it.

The Queen came too, of course. Carrying her pocketbook. I was in Ireland working and missed the party. "Ireland," Harry said. "You're dumping the Queen for... Ireland? What will I tell my mother?"

The Duchess was indeed appalled and pouted during my next visit, but still asked me to sign the guest book before I left. Syon House guest books went back centuries, and she and I had a ritual of standing in the hall gossiping about Harry as I signed. "Do you think he is any better? Is he taking his medicine?" That sort of thing.

I was in a hurry that morning. With the Duchess trailing behind me, I signed my name with a flourish. Right below someone called Elizabeth R. Who was she to take up almost the entire page, I thought.

"**Elizabeth Regina,**" the Duchess whimpers. "That's how the Queen signs her name. And Phyllis," she sighs, "the Queen gets her own page."

If I wasn't Harry's only confidante, I would have been banned from the castle. No way to fix it. The Duchess wasn't about to tear it out. What a mess.

# It's still the most embarrassing moment of my life.

# NOTES FROM THE FIELD
# MY PEOPLE

Otherwise known as associate producers,
fixers, drivers, translators, and interns.
Usually unpaid interns. I started that way.
It's a scam but a great way to learn.

They research, they organize, they get directions,
the best ones are a tad OCD. I look for that when I
hire them. I tell them that I plan to take advantage
of it and when they leave me, they should get some
therapy. I'll even pay for the first session. Ask Doug
Spiro—he'll tell you; I told him exactly that. And
oh, he was good. Went on to be a kick-ass producer
who I still love and admire. The world of television
could not function without these folks. And yet
most people outside of the biz barely know they
exist. If they get credit, it's in the part of the show
where you get up to pee or turn it off. And yet...
there would be no production without them.

Oh, okay, there could be, and these days there often is, but it's much, much tougher.

I started to list folks by name but there are hundreds and surely, I'd forget someone. And that is unforgiveable.

More than a dozen folks who worked at Ward and Associates or interned with me in earlier times went on to become hot-shit folks. Pretty quickly I made people sign an agreement that they would always take my phone calls. Even if they got Oprah famous. Just a precaution. Working for Ward and Associates was fun, or at least I tried to make it fun. On occasion I would kidnap whoever was at the office and take them on an adventure. A private ride on the carousel at Glen Echo Park was one. Or a visit to Whistler's Peacock Room at the Freer Museum. The best was kidnapping the seven people in the office that day to get manicures. When they got home every female partner noticed, and none of the male partners did. Ha!

I had one iron-clad rule: AS ADVERTISED.

This place is as advertised, which means that if I have a problem with you, you will hear it from me first. And I expect the same respect in return. Oh, I don't mean I think your haircut is too short or you hate my new shoes.

But if you complain about working late to others and not to me, you are breaking our deal. And if I tell anyone I don't think you are carrying your load before I have told you, I am absolutely not AS ADVERTISED.

If we all agree to be as advertised, then working at Ward and Associates is a safe place. See how that works?

This cartoon is by the now famous Nick Galifianakis who illustrates the Washington Post advice columnist Carolyn Hax. They are now syndicated in over 200 papers.

Nick was once my intern at WJLA TV in Washington when he gave me this drawing. It's one of my proudest possessions.

And I'm sure Nick would take my phone call, if I could find his number.

## Am I lucky or what?

# A SOUVENIR STORY

## LAST MINUTE CHRISTMAS SHOPPING

Dinner plate from steakhouse in McGregor, Iowa.

It is just before Christmas, and I am savoring my three-olive martini at a steak house in McGregor, Iowa, just across the state line from the prison in Prairie du Chien, Wisconsin. My cameraman, soundman, and I have already been to Boston, New York, Baltimore, and Kansas on the child molesters tour. So far, it's been a tough trip.

I pitched this topic because I understand murder. I am, for instance, more than ready to take out the dry cleaner. And that red head at the DMV. So far, my darling husband Michael is still alive, but he knows his demise is still on my possible list. "I want to kill you," is a common enough thought. But "I want to molest you," what's that about?

So far, it's been about listening to sad men tell sad stories. "It's wrong," they begin. "It's an urge that overwhelms me. Some days I can control it, some days I can't. I've been locked up now for (fill in blank) years and my urges are still here. I hate myself. I need help." These men have obviously never met each other, but they all tell a version of the same story. It gives me pause. Are child molesters just evil? I do believe there are evil people. People who should be removed from the rest of us for our own safety. Maybe we could find a more humane place to lock them up but locked up they should be.

Who these people are and who decides, well, that's the tricky part. So far, these guys don't seem evil to me, but, even if they are, they are going to get out.

And without help, they are likely to offend again. Even with help, the stats aren't good. This is a good place to say that the men I am meeting are not violent. They have never been violent, and the psychiatrists who treat them don't think they ever will be violent. You may think that's a small distinction, but to these guys it's huge. Not surprisingly, very few scientists research the urges of child molesters. The handful who do piggyback onto the research methods of the much more socially acceptable science of sexual desire.

The gold standard for measuring sexual arousal in men is the penile plethysmograph, pictured below.

This contraption measures minute changes in the circumference of the penis. Any changes in size, even those not felt by the subject, are recorded while he views sexually suggestive or pornographic pictures or listens to audio tapes with descriptions of children being molested.

The band is so sensitive the penis's owner may not even notice his stirring erection. A computer charts his "degree of arousal to each stimulus." So far on our trip, this has meant a slide show that includes many varieties of sex and many varieties of vegetables, flowers, and clouds. Apparently, the latter are included as control slides—not everything can be arousing, can it?

The lights go down, the slide show begins, and we shoot a few dozen of the slides, knowing we will edit it so only flowers and vegetables will actually be shown on television. We then retreat to film the technician in the next room, fiddling while the subject fiddles, so to speak. By Wisconsin, our tour of these smelly rooms is getting to all of us. To me, at least, the evidence is piling up that some men truly are only excited by children. (Are men the only deviant ones here or is a vagina meter just less practical?) There are researchers like Dr. Fred Berlin at Johns Hopkins doing brain scans of molesters— maybe the urge to molest is a deficiency in their wiring. Doesn't it almost have to be a deficiency in their wiring? I mean, really, who would choose to get turned on only by kids?

So far on this trip, I have talked to about 60 child molesters, including a truck driver, a rabbi, a lawyer, a plumber, and an insurance man. Most of these men are in prison, but not all of them. A dozen have agreed to be on camera. In the finished documentary I will do my best to present the facts and let the viewer decide. That's my job. But what do *I* think?

I think it's five days before Christmas. I am exhausted. I have no presents.

"Is it possible to buy this plate?" I ask the waitress.
"You want to buy the plate? Where are you from, lady?"
Negotiations ensue and eventually the plate is mine. Lucky Michael, guess what Santa's bringing him?

## Next stop, California.

# ME AND MY BRAIN

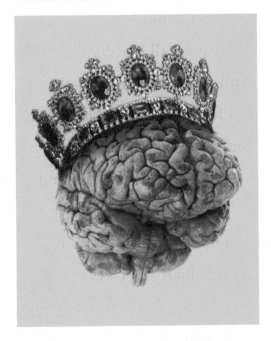

I come from a family of people who are bi-polar and depressive. And creative and imaginative. The researchers say they often go together. So, there's that.

This was a deep family secret. When I was a child, my mother was sometimes away getting ECT in the psych ward. Absolutely no one was to know. If we asked where she was, Dad just told us Mom was sick.

My amazingly creative younger brother also grew up struggling with his brain chemistry. Bill has been severely bi-polar all his life.

My father used so much energy keeping these secrets. I feel for all of us. How much easier it would have been to share the pain.

I too am bipolar and creative and imaginative. The first is medically true, the rest is my opinion. Depression first hit me hard at age 28, and I've been under a psychiatrist's care since then. I have what they call bi-polar 2, not as debilitating as bi-polar 1, which my mom and brother inherited.

The drugs have gotten much better over the years, but it's been a struggle for me. Especially when the seasons change and my SAD (Seasonal Affective Disorder) kicks in.

One of the joys of being an independent producer was it gave me the  cover to explore the latest research and interview the leading experts on mental illness.

It also gave me a platform for my documentaries and stories to help the general public understand the ubiquity of mental illness.

So, Ms. TV Producer got to do the first national story about Dr. Norman Rosenthal at the National Institute Mental Health (NIMH), who identified SAD.

I also sought out and reported stories on:

-OCD (obsessive compulsive disorder)

-Bi-polar 1 and 2—absolutely fascinating, to me anyway. The researchers at Johns Hopkins thought it might have survived evolution because as one said, "It's kind of like the warning lights on a car—too happy and too sad are both not great for survival. But seeing that far is often visionary." Still processing that one.


-A long-suffering woman on a brand-new drug for her stubborn depression. This was Prozac before it even had a name. Turned out it worked pretty well.

-Brain surgery on children with extreme seizures. These children had what's called a hemispherectomy—half of their brain was removed, and the remaining half compensated for many of their lost skills. How the brain rewired itself is remarkable in every way.

-Several stories on people with mental illness moving out of institutions and into group homes. And sometimes into homes of their own. What a process, for them and for us.

-One of our producers interviewed Oliver Sacks, the professor of neurology who did so much to make people aware of brain disorders with his book THE MAN WHO MISTOOK HIS WIFE FOR A HAT.

-Several stories on people with extreme phobias, defined as an irrational fear of things like snakes, heights, driving a car.

These phobias can cause panic attacks that can be paralyzing.

One woman was even terrified of signing her name—just think about that.

-People with agoraphobia, fear of leaving home.

-A fascinating story on Chris Sizemore, about the real-life person in the movie the THREE FACES OF EVE. Told you about Chris earlier.

-An investigative report on the abominable conditions of psychiatric hospitals in Mexico City. Truly inhumane.

-Dr. Candace Pert, a brilliant neuroscientist who helped discover a fundamental element of brain chemistry. Her book, *Molecules of Emotion: The Science Between Mind-Body Medicine*, lays out how groundbreaking this research is.

-Dr. Martin Seligman, who developed the now well-known theories of positive psychology and learned helplessness.

There are more. But you get the idea. The brain still interests me. One of the great things about working for yourself is you can follow your curiosity.

And if you are lucky, people will hire you to follow your nose.

I kept my personal struggles very much to myself until a few decades ago. Bad for business, scary to folks, breaking family rules.

But my friends in the Disability Rights Movement were speaking out. I should, too.

Now I'll tell you happily. What would you like to know?

Here's an example of how much the world is changing. Or maybe how much change is needed. A few years ago, a friend died suddenly. Was it an accidental drug overdose or suicide? She struggled with her demons; we knew that.

Months later I decided to talk about her death at a party I give annually for interesting women.

A friend and I had carefully sourced and collected pamphlets about how to talk to depressed and suicidal people. And where to get help in our immediate area. There were about 60 people at the party.

I stood up talked about our friend's struggles and we had a toast in her honor. Then I spoke to people about my own struggles. And then I asked people to raise their hands if they or anyone they knew had struggled with mental illness. About 20 or 30 hands were raised. Some haltingly.

It was surprising and powerful. And out in the open.

A person I didn't know, who had arrived late, was still shell-shocked from her husband's suicide just a three weeks earlier. She didn't raise her hand, but I knew who she was and later introduced her to a dear friend whose husband had committed suicide a few years back. They were actually standing next to each other in the hallway.

Both women were so comforted to meet another woman who had been through it. Serendipity rocks.

After I sat down, people mingled. At least two dozen women quietly thanked me, telling me they too struggled with some form of mental illness or had it in their immediate family.

Women paired up on the deck to talk amongst themselves. Later, two different people took me to lunch to tell me their stories. And thank me. They felt less alone.

And at the end of the party all the pamphlets were gone.

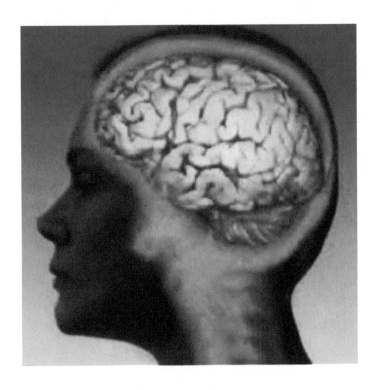

Maybe we have finally reached a tipping point where mental illness is becoming just that, an illness.

**Okay, maybe not quite. But we're getting there.**

**Go ahead, ask me anything.**

# WORDS TO LIVE BY

Just remember, we're all in this alone.

Lily Tomlin

# ENOUGH WITH THE PITY ALREADY

Here's a story about my wonderful friend, Jimmy (James) DePreist. It illustrates to me how far the Americans with Disabilities Act has changed our country. And how far we still have to go.

James DePreist conducts

I met Jimmy when he was the associate conductor of the National Symphony Orchestra in DC. I was the media director of the Falls Church City Schools and took my darlings to the symphony to make a video. Somehow Jimmy and I became lifelong friends. Pretty cool, huh?

Growing up in Philadelphia, Jimmy and his mother Ethel lived next door to his Aunt Marian. Aunt Marian was the famous contralto, Marian Anderson. In 1939, she was barred from performing at Constitution Hall by the Daughters of the American Revolution because of the color of her skin.

There was an uproar. First Lady Eleanor Roosevelt resigned from the DAR in protest. A few weeks later, with Eleanor's help, Marian Anderson sang for a large crowd of 75,000 on the steps of the Lincoln Memorial. Millions more listened on their radios. The Secretary of the Interior introduced Anderson to the integrated crowd by saying, "In this great auditorium under the sky, all of us are free."

It became a defining moment of the civil rights movement.

Aunt Marian was Jimmy's hero, his best friend, and his mentor. He was a musical child, but his aunt's talent was daunting. How could he compete with that? Not possible to even consider following in her footsteps, he told me.

His mom wanted Jimmy to be a lawyer. He dutifully studied economics at Wharton, even got a Master's in Communication, but eventually told mom no to lawyering. Not that he had a plan of his own.

Music was in his blood. Jimmy and his friends had fun with the "Jimmy DePreist Jazz Quintet" he organized in college. In 1962, Aunt Marian got his group booked on a good will tour of the Near and Far East.

On a stop in Thailand, the King, on a whim, asked Jimmy if he wanted to conduct his Bangkok orchestra. YES, he said. He jumped at the opportunity and loved it. That night, he told me, he went to bed saying to himself, to hell with not competing with Aunt Marian, I'm going to conduct. Not that he fully understood this at the time, mind you.

But within days he woke up unable to get out of bed.

Huh?

It was polio.

Aunt Marian soon arranged for a ride home on a military transport with wounded Vietnam soldiers.

In the months it took to treat his polio and slowly recover, Jimmy fell in love with and eventually married his nurse, Ginette. And more good news, the doctors said he would eventually be able to walk with leg braces and the metal canes called Canadian crutches.

As soon as possible, Jimmy excitedly took up the baton. He was good. After winning a prestigious conducting competition, he was hired by Leonard Bernstein as associate conductor of the New York Symphony. Jimmy's conducting career took off.

The man was talented.

Jimmy made his highly acclaimed European debut with the Rotterdam Philharmonic in 1969 and went on to an international career.

He became associate conductor of the National Symphony in DC, music director of the Quebec Symphony Orchestra and the Oregon Symphony Orchestra, and a guest conductor at orchestras around the world. He also made over 50 recordings with the Oregon Symphony Orchestra.

In 2005, Jimmy was awarded the Presidential Medal of the Arts. He also wrote two books of poetry. Not bad. Not bad at all.

As Jimmy wandered the world, the two of us stayed in touch. I sent him research about how conductors die old because they swing their arms so much, they get good cardio workouts. I was also the cheeky friend who continued to give him grief about not wanting to compete with Aunt Marian.

Me: "Go full tilt man, don't hang back!"

Him: "You're right, you're right."


Aunt Marian moved in with Jimmy toward the end of her life. It was precious time for both of them.

When she died in 1993, I called Jimmy up and asked him if he could now walk. She's not competition anymore, ya know?

He laughed. Said, "Only you Phyllis. Only you."

So what does this have to do with disability attitudes, you are asking? In 1996, Ward and Associates was hired to produce MY COUNTRY, which aired on PBS.

It is a one-hour documentary about attitudes towards people with disabilities. And how they are too often excluded from American life. Too often regarded as objects of pity.

Even though the Americans with Disabilities Act was passed in 1990 we still have a long way to go with attitudes.

My original thought was to get the great violinist Itzhak Pearlman to host. He had contracted polio when he was four and like Jimmy, walked with Canadian crutches. Itzhak had hosted one of our earlier ADA films and was the obvious choice.

When asked about his disability during an NPR interview, Itzhak said it has no effect on his performance. "I can't walk very well, but I'm not onstage to do walking," he told NPR's Steve Inskeep. "I'm on the stage to play."

And then... it occurs to me... Jimmy is perfect! He has a great voice. We can start the show with him standing in front of the Lincoln Memorial, telling us the Aunt Marian story, and showing clips of her concert in 1939.

Then Jimmy can stand in front of Constitution Hall, telling us it took another 50 years, not until the passing of the ADA, for the hall to become accessible. (Footnote: Racial barriers came down in 1952.)
Brilliant!

But would he do it?

Him: I don't know Phyllis. I'm not really into highlighting my disability.

(Huh?)

Him: Oh, I agree with you, but I just don't want to remind people.

Me: But you're damn proud of being Black.
Him: Of course, I am.

Sooooo. Jimmy was proud to be Black but was less than thrilled about being seen as disabled. Apparently, a lot of people with disabilities feel this way, somehow vaguely ashamed. Most of them aren't even aware of it.

Him: Let me think about it.

Me: If YOU haven't accepted your disability, I say to him, how the hell are we supposed to?

A call from Itzhak, and an overnight think changed his mind.

I'm in, he says. Enthusiastically even. Sort of.

Jimmy did a great job.

Those of us who worked on MY COUNTRY are very proud of it. And of him.

Itzhak and Jimmy performing together

And the people in the documentary, not pitiful or heroic. Just people.
GOT IT?

**Footnote:** James DePriest died at his home in Scottsdale, Arizona on Friday, February 8, 2013. He was 76. We loved each other very much. His friendship was one of the great privileges of my life. You can watch MY COUNTRY online through ADA.gov. Go to the website and search for MY COUNTRY.

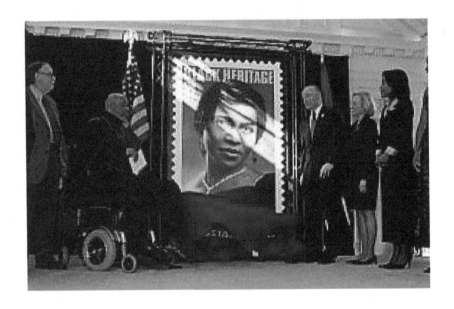

# PRODUCER ADVICE FOR EDITING
## KILL YOUR DARLINGS

Oh what a tough lesson to learn. Ah, the editing room…A haven.

A place to regroup after the exhaustion of the field. We now have a script and hours and hours of video, hard gathered over many miles, often in several countries. I'm bringing them to you, Ms. Editwoman. Or Editman. To make them come alive. To work your magic. To work civilized hours inside with coffee and lunch nearby. Oh, who wouldn't love to edit?

What's that you say? The first cut is an hour and 26 minutes? Impossible.

It is, huh? Okay, let's go through it together. If it occurs to us to cut it, we cut it. Agree?

Much better. That only took two days. How long is it now? Still six minutes long? Well shit.

Let's sleep on it and try again tomorrow.

Okay, we slept on it. There's nothing left to cut. Nothing. Whaaaa? We can't cut that! Are you kidding me? It took us an entire day to get to that location, and another day to talk them into letting us shoot.

Do you have any idea how much time and money we spent on this scene? NO. No way. Besides, I love it. It gives such character to the story.

Brings a sense of the countryside to life.

It's one of my very favorite parts. NO, we can't cut that. NO WAY.

Let's sleep on it.

OK, we slept on it. I was up half the night. I LOVE that scene. LOVE IT.

I'm not rational, you say? Maybe you're right. Maybe it's not essential to the storyline.

Maybe it IS a darling of mine.

Let's sleep on it.

Why do we always have to get rid of the parts I love the most? Ruthless.

Okkaaayyyy... Cut it. Arrrggghhhhhhh.

RESULT: It seems our cut is now at time. When we screen it for the powers that be, they jump on the jump cut, but never even noticed my missing darling. No one did. Heartbreaking.

**KILLING YOUR DARLINGS** is the

toughest part of any edit.

It just is.

# EXIT

"I've given up on dying," my mom said.

"You're going to live forever?"

"No, but I was so hoping I was dying soon. I guess that's not going to happen."

She's 87 and impatient. I'm not. I'm not impatient at all.

**Pat Hippe**

Michael's dad died just days after his 102<sup>nd</sup> birthday.

**Joe Ward**

He played poker with his great grandkids the day of his birthday party and told us all to start planning next year's festivities. The very next day, though, he told Michael he'd decided enough was enough. It took him just ten days to die. That's not uncommon, according to Elizabeth Kubler Ross, the death and dying guru. She'd been at the bedside of over 10,000 deaths, she told me, and knew a thing or two about exiting.

## Dr. Elisabeth Kübler-Ross

Wikipedia: *Elizabeth Kübler-Ross was the first individual to transfigure the way that the world looks at the terminally ill. She pioneered hospice care, palliative care, and near-death research, and was the first to bring terminally ill individuals' lives to the public eye. Kübler-Ross was the driving force behind the movement for doctors and nurses alike to "treat the dying with dignity." Her extensive work with the dying led to the 1969 internationally best-selling book On Death and Dying where she first discussed her theory of the five stages of grief.*

I knew her work well and was thrilled to get a chance to interview her. Elizabeth contends each of us choose the moment of our death. "Terminally ill children," she says, "almost always send their bereft and exhausted parents away for a short break and then die while they are gone. The child feels guilty for letting them down and so dying while Mom and Dad are out of the room is the only way the child can let go. I've seen it hundreds of times."

I interviewed Elizabeth on her farm in Virginia. My dad was dying at the time. I told her my dad and I didn't really talk. It's a long story but we hadn't been close for at least 15 years.

"Go see him right now," Elizabeth ordered. "It doesn't matter if he wants to see you. Sending flowers to funeral parlors is too late. Bring flowers to the hospital, and if he won't see you, throw the flowers into his room. When he dies, you'll thank me."

**Gillman Hippe**

She was right. Instead of flowers, I took one of those temporary tattoos of Bill Clinton. Dad hated Bill Clinton and laughed. It was okay after that. More than okay really. When I returned the next day, he happily showed me the tattoo, which was now on his butt. "Clinton's finally kissing my ass," he said.

I told Dad that Kubler Ross insists dying is fun. "If you're not having fun, you're not dying," I told him.

For the next three weeks, I called him every day from wherever I was to ask him if he was having fun yet. I even managed a call from the middle of the Atlantic Ocean, where I was doing a story on trans-Atlantic cables. (Oh joy.)

"Hey, Dad, are you having fun yet?" "Nope." "Then you're not dying." It became our way of reconnecting. After so many years, we were both amazed. I truly think he stuck around a few extra days to see if I would keep calling. One morning, *he* called me. This is our entire conversation: "The fat lady is singing. I love you. Tell Michael hello."

Dad was literally at death's door but managed to call five of his six children to say goodbye. The sixth—my brother Rob—was sitting by his bedside and somehow Dad was too macho to talk to him in person. My mother knew Rob would never forgive his father—he was, after all, the one who handed the phone to Dad to make the five other calls.

In a stroke of brilliance, Mom told Rob to go out into the driveway and call Dad from his cell phone. Upon which Dad happily told Rob he loved him.

He died a few hours later. Men, huh?

It was nearly the perfect death, if any death can be called perfect. Most people aren't that lucky.

The toughest deaths, I think, are the sudden ones. Elizabeth told me a remarkable story about a young woman who'd been in a car crash in Los Angeles. A Good Samaritan knelt by her side as they waited for the ambulance. "Please tell Mom I'm with Dad, we're fine," she said. He promised he would. And then she died.

Two hours later, the Good Samaritan tracked down her mother on the East Coast and tenderly broke the news.

Mom started sobbing, which isn't the least bit surprising. She asked the time of the accident.

Through her tears she told him that her husband had died of a massive heart attack less than an hour before her daughter died.

Mom had been trying to reach her daughter.
How can this possibly be?

Is death as inscrutable as most of us assume? Is it part of a chaotic universe, or an orderly one? Or both?

Here is a fact I find both hard to believe and very comforting: Physicists says that here on earth matter can't be created or destroyed. Huh? I first heard this at a very dear friend's funeral many years ago. All of our atoms are still around?

With one small exception. Apparently a very few of our atoms are radioactive and escape out into the universe.

But most of our atoms get recycled right here on earth. Yep. Look it up, it's true.

**In Elizabeth's experience, and mine, death is full of mystery never neatly wrought. For now, at least, I prefer to delay.**

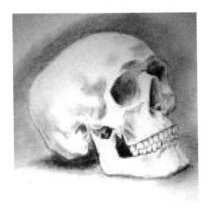

Footnote: Mom didn't die until she was 94.

# WORDS TO LIVE BY
# MY ATTITUDE

"Everything can be taken from a person but one
thing: the last of the human freedoms—
To choose one's attitude in any given set of
circumstances."
**Viktor Frankl**
Referring to his time in the concentration camps.

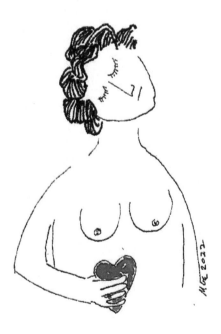

# FACTOIDS I LOVE

# GRIEF

# RESEARCH SAYS HAVE ONE
# REALLY GOOD BAD DAY

My best grieving advice—

Perhaps you have already done it. If not, all the research says this really helps.

As soon as possible, have one REALLY GOOD BAD DAY.

Be as self-indulgent as you can possibly be.

Swear, throw things, curse the gods, drink heavily, call anyone and everyone and tell them what assholes they are and that you don't deserve this shit. That you are sooooo nice and they are suuuuchh shits and how can this be happening?

Eat ice cream from the tub. **DO NOT FEEL GUILTY** about anything at all.

Did I say throw things?

An entire 24 hours of pity. Anger. Wrath. Yep, Wrath. Don't be talked down by anyone.

Oh how it helps.

> **"In three words I can sum up everything I've learned about life:**
> **It goes on."** *Robert Frost*

# NEARNESS TO GREATNESS
## JOHN GLENN

I interviewed Glenn several times in my life as a television producer. The best was for a piece on Sally Ride, who at the time was about to become the first woman astronaut. John was less than impressed. Didn't have much to say and so I wandered into things I wanted to know. Me: So, John, what was the most amazing sight you saw in space?

Him: Well, Phyllis, honestly it was my pee.

It crystallized the minute it hit space and I watched out the little window. It was amazingly beautiful.

NASA Public library

**Yep, that was John's story and he stuck to it.**

**Nearness to greatness indeed.**

RIP John Glenn. July 18, 1921-December 8, 2016

# MY RETIREMENT PLAN

My retirement plan has always been prison. Lots of time to read, free rent, medical care, new friends. And you get to unload a lot of anger and frustration getting in.

I'm serious. Ask anyone who knows me. They'll tell you. Back when we had a television production company, all I had to do was whisper I was thinking of retiring and everyone in the place hopped to. I never said it lightly.

That and the shark. They still talk about the shark.

It was a blow-up shark that traveled the world with me. I only blew it up when things were royally and truly fucked. Usually in the middle of a shoot on the Masaii Mara when the giraffes didn't show up at sunset for the first time ever. "Really, Phyllis, EVER!" Or the apparently now legendary time when I laid my shark gently on the desk of the news director of NBC. Things were not going well for Jane Pauley and me and our documentary on the East German Sports Machine. This was right after the Berlin Wall fell and we had amazing stuff. Except the NBC dude in charge of us didn't seem to care about facts. Forced me to go over his head with the shark. Yep, it's a legend.

Anyway, as I was saying. Prison is a good plan. Especially if you're a freelance television producer who is always fronting your next project with money from your last. When we moved to the Eastern Shore of Virginia in 2000, I immediately began surveying my retirement options.

The local jail seemed nice, actually. But how to get in when I needed to?

Now realize there are only about 40,000 people on the Eastern Shore. And everyone seems pleasant enough. What crime would I commit?

My first thought was to hold up the toll booth lady at the Chesapeake Bay Bridge Tunnel. Nope, not enough cash to get any real time. Even I could see that. And she always gives the dogs treats. How could I mess with her?

My next idea was to rob the local bank. We go in to set up our account and I explain my dilemma to the nice lady at Sun Trust. "Oh," she says. "Not a bad idea, but you need to rob a bigger bank. Ours is too small, we don't keep enough money. Try the one in Belle Haven, that might work." See why I like it here? Everyone is so helpful.

Hmmmmm... this isn't going to be as easy as I thought.

And then my friend Pat sends me articles about how prisons are overcrowded, and they are giving out shorter sentences and letting people out early. We always planned to retire together. She lobbies for disability rights, and you KNOW there's no money in that. And we always planned to share a cell. At least I did. Pretty naïve, huh? I think Pat knew it doesn't work that way.

Even the three strikes and you're out laws are softening up. Is my plan too late?

And then I see a local judge at a Christmas party. He says he's sorry to tell me but I really am going to have to kill someone to get any real time. Shit. I turn to my darling husband standing with us and say, "Sorry darling." "Oh no," says the judge, "killing Michael would be justifiable homicide." (Need I say Michael is a lawyer?) As he's leaving the party, the judge finds me and whispers. "Ask for a bench trial. I'll see what I can do."

## Oh I love this place.

# FACTOIDS I LOVE
## It's called the UBEND Curve
## Another factoid TV research brought
## me that cheers me up every day

The U-Bend Theory is very simple. It says our happiness tends to follow a U-shape from early adulthood to old age. People's highest levels of happiness generally come at the beginning and later stretches of our adult life, with the lowest levels in the middle.

I love this factoid. Found out about it a decade ago and it helps my attitude tremendously. The best is yet to come.

Researchers say: "Although the typical age for hitting the bottom dip in the U-bend varies from country to country, 46 is the global average."
Makes sense. Around then, you realize you're probably not going to be president. And even worse, you don't want to be.

I dove into this research headfirst, just my kind of information. And yes, they have replicated this worldwide.

Let me repeat: Many say our twenties are the most happy, slowly descending to that 46 to 50 low point of lifetime happiness and then creeping up to highest happiness again between 83-85 and later.

**BRING IT ON!**

**Brought to you as a public service, click away**

**yourself**

**for more research.**

Oh, I love factoids.

# MY CULTURAL CONFUSION

## Me and the Earl   Part Four
## The Sun Gets In Your Eyes
## 1978

"Oh, Harry," say I. "You're squinting."

We've been sitting in the Red Drawing Room having afternoon tea and enjoying having the place to ourselves. The place being Syon House, his family's London home.

If you've read this far, you already know Harry Percy is the Earl of Northumberland. And, as you know, I have been living here while traveling in and out of the city for my television directing job. Harry says it is near the airport and convenient. He is right.

We are blissfully content this fall day, casually sitting in opulence, looking out the windows, and watching the sun sink over the grounds.

We are looking out the window on the bottom floor, to the right of the door.

And here's a picture of Harry on the grounds in front of his Greenhouse.

I have many Harry stories to tell but this one is about my moment of insight on this glorious fall afternoon. A moment when you understand something that you really didn't. They are fairly rare in life, and I treasure them.

For starters, in all of Syon's 200 acres of historic wonderment, there wasn't one place to sit outside and enjoy the breeze. I mean, really?

The house was built in the 1500s and in all of these years nobody ever wanted to sit outside? Or were all the servants who used to make that happen now gone? A small deck and a lawn chair were out of the question, I suppose.

As I've said, Harry and I liked each other. And spent lots of time together that year. He was a sad man. Living in the world of lost kingdoms. And smart enough to know he was superfluous.

He would repeat things like: "If we hadn't lost the Battle of Hastings in 1066, I would be king."

"How sad for you," I would again reply.

Like many great houses, Syon has become a tourist attraction, allowing visitors to tour the great rooms, the greenhouse, and the garden and then have a very posh lunch in the newly opened restaurant aimed at the well-heeled. "Running a great house is an expensive proposition," and "God help us, we aren't about to sell a Van Dyke. Maybe a Whistler if we get desperate."

We settled side by side in a banquette, sipping our claret and watching the only other people in the place—a Middle Eastern family headed by an Arab sheik whose name and country I have forgotten.

The women and children sat at one table, bodyguards at another, the sultan and his brothers at the third. Thirty people or so eating lobster and having a grand old time. The waiter said they came every Sunday for lunch. It must have cost a bundle.

Harry just stared. I'd never seen him so angry. "People like me should still be running the world," he said, "not these upstart Arabs with no manners and questionable breeding. All they did was find oil. They're powerful by happenstance, not history."

He actually talked like this.

"Don't you think you're being a little racist?" I said.

We ate in silence after that while Harry sulked. I tried to see things from his perspective, but really, he just needed to get over himself. Redecorate maybe, I suggested. Bring in some mid-century modern to refresh the place. Or move out and live a little—rent a loft in London or go rafting in some remnant of the empire.

But we both knew that would never happen. Harry lived frozen in time.

That afternoon, the two of us sat in the sumptuous but chilly drawing room, nibbling our stale Fig Newtons. Slurping our cold tea.

"Oh, Harry," says I. "You're squinting."

The glare from the setting sun was in Harry's eyes.

He rang for a servant to close the shutter. This involved getting up, ringing a bell, waiting long minutes for the long-suffering butler to shuffle upstairs from the servant's quarters, and then fussing at him to close the shutters to the exact angle he desired.

"Geez, Harry, why don't you just get up and do it yourself," I said.

"Never occurred to me," he answered.

And there it was, my moment of insight. The man had no agency with the world. No realization that he, Harry Percy, could actually make something happen of his own accord. That he, Harry Percy, could get up and make the sun go away. In so many ways he felt helpless. It is a terrible thing, this.

Harry was an extreme case,
but after that afternoon with Harry, I was
never again jealous of great wealth or great
celebrity.

# NOTES FROM THE FIELD
# OVERTIME
# OH JOY

"Hello, everybody, it's me again, Gino. It's 5 p.m. here in the trauma center. Hour ten and still no traumas. Just want you to know we are doing our part to keep children safe."

We have been camped here at Children's Hospital in DC for many days now, shooting a documentary on the Golden Hour of trauma care. Did I say shooting? I meant to say waiting. Day 11 and still no traumas, in a hospital that has over 1,800 a year. Gino (cameraman) has taken to announcing the lack of action on the hospital PA system every hour we are here. It's become very popular.

As for me? Ugh. After eight hours of non-shooting, it's now time-and-a-half to continue just sitting here waiting. It's called overtime.

And oh, how crews love it. I've heard stories of crews casually wiping their brows with twenty-dollar bills to let their producer know their joy. So subtle.

"Of course, we want this story as much as you do, Phyllis. Of course, we do. We're professionals like you."

But when exactly do I pull the plug? Leave now and we have spent a day's shoot for nothing. This trauma documentary has been killer, so to speak. We have been shooting it here and at the Baltimore Trauma Center. At least four times now, as we packed up after a long night and pulled away to drive back to DC, we look out our van window to see ambulances arriving with trauma patients.

By the time we could possibly repark, unpack, and get upstairs we would have missed our story. Frustration is a four-letter word.

"Let's skip tomorrow, guys. I need a night off."

"Oh, you should have been here last night!" says the trauma doc as we arrive on Thursday. "There was a train wreck. Twelve people brought here in bad shape."

Arrggghhhhhh.

Here is the deal with overtime. It's a lot like life. When is enough enough? Getting the story may seem easy when you watch it on TV

Gathering it can be easy, but more often a series of judgements that no one knows the answers to. When that asshole cameraman told me that producers were as useless as tits on a bull, he was totally full of bull. Making decisions on the spot is unrelenting and constant. I NEED THAT SUNSET! I will pay overtime to get it.

And then in the editing room, there isn't time for the sunset, it doesn't fit the story and it's a darling I won't give up. Do you know how much overtime that damn sunset cost?

Knowing when to pull the plug on a job, a marriage, a friendship. When it's time to go home and when to stay another half hour at the bar to keep talking to this scintillating woman. Oops. Tipsy.

It's been a lifetime fascination of mine. This timing thing. Why is today the day? Yesterday, I tried to change but it just didn't happen. Today it was easy. Why???? Okay, let's stay to get the shot. Okay, let's pack up and go home. To this day, no idea how to get it right.

**OVERTIME TWO:** My British crew and I had a miserable day chasing snakes in Mombasa. Black mambas to be exact, one of the world's deadliest. Mark, the snake catcher, went into remote villages looking for them in the thatched roofs where they often hid out. He milked them and sold the venom. I should mention that my earliest childhood memory is as a toddler sitting on a copperhead along the side of a road in Missouri.

Four adults above me screaming as the snake bit me. To this day I am beyond scared of snakes of any kind.

Black mambas, well you can imagine. Why am I here?

I am a producer and producers produce. Poor Nick (camera) is looking through his black and white viewfinder trying to find the snake on a thatched roof. Thank God he is British. Gino would have quit on the spot. "Let me get this straight. Black and white viewfinder. Thatched roof. Black mamba. You are out of your mind, woman."

Later that day, I am trying to capture the last snake story and get Mark out of my life. The spitting cobra won't spit. We are exhausted. Emotionally drained. And it's about to be overtime.

I need one more shot of the damn snake spitting into the camera. "How do I make him spit," I ask?

"Wave a white handkerchief in front of him," says Mark.

"Huh?"

I stand three feet in front of the damn snake and wave the damn handkerchief.

Snake looks directly into the camera and spits at me.

Producers produce, right? Get me out of here.

Overtime. Oh joy.

# ANOTHER IN A SERIES OF
# SOUVENIR STORIES
## East Germany, 1990

I see it first, but that doesn't mean much. She is Jane Pauley and I am not. Except this is East Germany in 1990, just after the wall comes down. Jane's celebrity doesn't seem to have penetrated the concrete and barbed wire. We have finagled our way into the newsroom of the East German newspaper Berliner Zeitung.

It is two days before the first free elections, and we are both hiding in the closet to get out of the camera's way. It's dusty and hot in here and Jane is so very much not a person who has ever hidden from a camera.

She has recently been replaced on the TODAY SHOW by Deborah Norville. Viewers loudly and immediately revolted. "That nice Jane Pauley with her unfortunate hair has been tossed out by that vixen." Many people in the halls of NBC think the very network is now in peril. And the network is suddenly frantic to showcase Jane as a serious journalist with her own big deal prime time special.

So, Jane has been here in East Germany for five days now, strategically inserting herself into the footage we have been shooting for weeks before she arrived. It's an hour documentary about the East German sports machine—of which I have plenty to tell you if you are the least bit interested.

Here we are, Jane and I, in the back closet of the newspaper still run by the secret police.

A few months from now, the Stasi editor will be removed, but in March 1990 the newspaper is still a mouthpiece for Communism.

Not a place you'd expect to see Christmas. But there it is, a traditional Black Forest candle holder with nutcrackers and angels and a tree.

Jane and I have been hiding here while Gino (camera) and Craig (sound) are shooting the newsroom in action. I found it lying on back shelf in the closet. What's this? Isn't this a Communist country? Isn't that an angel?

I drag the candleholder out of the back closet.

"Oh that," says the newspaper editor, "...it's nothing...sentimental...silly... but best to keep it tucked away. We sneak it out at Christmas. Please, if you like it take it. It's meaningless."

Yes! I say.

Yes! Jane says.

But I found it, I say.

But, but… says Jane. But!

It was quite the trip. And Jane's first assignment after leaving the TODAY SHOW. We were reporting on the East German Sports Machine, as it was called—the state sponsored system that produced so many medals for East Germany at the Olympics.

**Gino reaching through the wall to shake hands in the east**

It was an historic time to be there. Each day confirmed long-rumored doping practices and unveiled new secret strategies for winning. And we were there first.

The day she arrived, Jane and I watched Katarina Witt, East Germany's gold medal glamour girl, skate for us in a dungeon of a rink, a crumbling cement block. It was disheartening.

Among other stories we reported:

1. Every five-year-old East German child was screened for athletic ability. If their skeletal structure and reflexes were promising, they were taken from their parents and sent to special schools to train.

Jane interviewed Heinrich, an Olympic skier, about his gold medal run. Heinrich had quite literally grown up in the sports machine.

School for these lucky few is training and more training, with two or three hours of real school thrown in. Heinrich told us that even as a seven-year-old, he knew that the small blue "vitamins" on his breakfast tray made him special. (They were steroids.) "They are given to only the most talented kids at boarding school, almost everybody else gets the pink ones," he told us. The most talented kids were very carefully monitored by a team of top scientists and had a chance of leading a very privileged life in this poor, communist country.

2. Before competitions, the coaches stopped the steroids in time for the athletes to pass the drug tests.

What the athletes called the "piss car" would crisscross the countryside collecting urine samples to be sure they were drug free enough for the competitions. "When we were older," Heinrich said, "and if you were good enough to compete, the 'piss car' would come to collect your pee." It was an efficient way to make sure the doping has been halted in time to clear the athlete's bodies. Testing before the tests, as it were.

3. Athletes who would benefit from high altitude training (skiers, for example) were not allowed out of the country to train. Defection was too much of a risk. In the potentially headline-making part of our filming, we were the first media of any kind to see the giant hyperbaric chamber hidden at the end of a country road. Stasi guards control the entrance and troll the grounds to keep everyone out... and everyone in.

Its existence was such a state secret that even the guards' families had no idea what they were guarding. The chamber was buried in dirt, only a small door led to acres of underground space. Giant turbines pumped out the sour air, allowing elite athletes to train at simulated high altitudes without ever leaving the country. One too many Alpine defections.

We descend to find maybe a hundred athletes
training in a dozen sports. The space is overcome
with fluorescent lighting, decades of stale sweat and
noisy coaches. Only the best of the best train in this
grim chamber 10 to 12 hours a day. They stay in
nearby barracks, chaperoned by their coaches and
guarded by guys with rifles.

4. The scientists who designed the sports machine—and believe me it was truly a machine—believe that sex enhances performance. Coaches of both sexes, we are told, consider it part of their job description to fuck the elite athletes the night before their event. Is this true? I have no idea, but we hear it half a dozen times and maybe it is. They won't say it on camera though.

(This was a state mandate, mind you, not a rogue Larry Nassar.)

It was an exhausting trip, but an exciting one, full of new reporting.

Gino, Craig and I were there a month, living together in a one-bathroom apartment that the crew considered squalor. Oh please.

The on-site fixers were terrific. As usual, the stories couldn't have been done without them.

Jane came for a week. She was a trouper.

We were all very proud of what we accomplished. Jane and I stayed in touch afterwards.

But our documentary never aired. To this day I have no idea why.

I have theories, of course. Most likely internal politics at NBC having to do with how the network wanted to position Jane. Her next gig was a short-lived talk show.

For Gino, Craig, and me it was heartbreaking. To have our efforts to go unreported was awful.

**But we had an amazing adventure.**
**And I have a very special Christmas candleholder.**

This Black Forest Christmas treasure sits in my window now—a black silhouette in the morning sun. It was given to me by the editor of the Berliner Zeitung. Celebrity only goes so far, right? I did see it first. Or maybe I was just closer. I'm positive I was the one who asked about it.

**Sorry, Jane, it's mine.**

# MY CULTURAL CONFUSION
# THE SWORDMAKER'S
# WORKSHOP
# ADVENTURES IN JAPAN
# PART TWO

Muroran, Japan 1986

"Stop. Just stop," I say, louder than I intend.

For months there has been tension between Kevin, my lanky 6'2" cameraperson, and my Japanese crew of producer, soundman, gaffer, and translator. Kevin is from New York and very good at his job.

For months now, the five of us have been crisscrossing this island country on our own. And struggling to communicate.

Let's just stipulate that a tall American woman who smokes cigars telling short Japanese men what to do is not a formula for success.

"Ishida-san," I say, "I don't understand why you are doing what you are doing. Please help me understand."

What he is doing is putting up every light in his very big arsenal of lights to flood every inch of this very small space with high noon nuance. As in none. As usual.

Whether it is a huge factory floor, or this tiny charcoal fired studio, Ishida-san must make it glow bonfire bright.

It drives Kevin nuts. About a month ago, I negotiated a just-in-time compromise. A good one, if I do say so myself. The tension between them was making all of us miserable.

New rules. Ishida-san will now haul out his haul. Spend forever setting up every damn light. Go for it. Fuss away.

Meanwhile Kevin will pace outside, smoking his cigarettes, wondering why the fuck he is here.

When the lights are up to Ishida-san's satisfaction, he will step outside while Kevin goes in and turns almost all of them off, rearranging the ones he wants to keep. Take your time.

A tender truce. But it is working.

Today we are going to shoot in the studio of Horii Tanetada, one of Japan's Living National Treasures. He is a swordsmith. It hasn't been easy to get to this place on this day to shoot this story. I am so looking forward to it.

# PROBLEM ONE:

Horii Tanetada lives on the northernmost Japanese island of Hokkaido, in the town of Muroran, on the outskirts of Sapporo. It has been a struggle to arrive, much less be admitted to the studio.

When we check into the local hotel, Kevin makes sure the camera has survived the bullet train ride. He discovers it has not.

It is now 4:40 in the afternoon. We are at least seven hours from Tokyo and any possibility of a replacement.

Kevin calls our Sony office and the person who answers the phone says he will be there with a new camera as soon as possible.

Many hours later, Kevin and I are still sitting on the rooftop of our hotel, watching the stars, and telling each other stories. We have had only each other to talk to for months now and the usual crew

hanging out topics have been long ago exhausted.

We are down to, "Tell me about the second time you got laid." Pitiful.

At 12:20 in the morning, the bedraggled messenger arrives with the camera. Kevin makes sure it works. We breathe easier, and Kevin asks him to please sit down and have a drink.

"I must go back immediately," he says.

"Oh, please, that is such a long trip. At least have a beer. Why can't you stay?"

"My wife is in labor. I must go back."

Huh?

"Couldn't someone else bring us the camera?" I ask incredulously.

I answered the phone," he says, as if it is obvious, "and so it is my duty to bring you the camera."

"Duty? Really?"

"Don't you understand?" the translator explained. "Haruto was the person walking by when you called.

He was the one who answered the phone and so it was his duty to bring the camera. It never would have occurred to him to ask someone else. Is it different in America?"

Sort of.

And off Haruto goes into the night.


**PROBLEM TWO:**

Horii, our swordsmith, absolutely won't allow a woman into his studio.

"IT IS NOT ALLOWED. This is a sacred space. My ancestors have used this studio for generations. Women are not allowed."

"Okay," I say. "No problem. Then you won't be on PBS."

## PROBLEM THREE:

"It takes months for me to forge a Katana sword," says Horrii. "I use at least twenty bags of this charcoal, which is made from special pine trees. I fold the molten steel onto itself at least twenty times over many weeks. When I am done, the blade will have a million layers. It is so very special."

"They have proven in a science lab that Katana swords do not rust even if you leave them in salt water," he says proudly.

"You will need to film all of this, beginning to end."

"Not gonna happen."

See problem two.

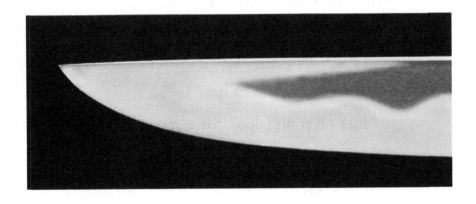

## PROBLEM FOUR:

Finally, here we all are, in Horii's small studio. The wooden walls are black with charcoal dust. Sunlight streams in through missing chinks in the wood. There's a barely contained inferno in the corner. And layers of smelting steel glowing red hot. An anvil. Two small windows pierce the darkness, leaving dancing dust in the air and patterns on the dirt floor.

Horii wears the swordsmith's traditional snowy white kimono signifying purity of spirit, he tells us. He looks magnificent.

Ishida-san starts dragging in his haul.

"Stop," I say. "Just stop."

Kevin is already outside, pouting and lighting up.

"Please help me understand why every light has to be on," I ask sincerely.

"Just stop and look for a moment before you start. Can you see the andirons in the corner with just your eyes?"

"Not really," says Ishida-san.

"Don't you see how beautiful the patterns of light on the floor are?"

"Not really."

"You don't see them, or they are not beautiful?"

"They are not beautiful."

"Ishida-san, I am really trying to understand. Have you never heard of the Impressionists? Doesn't Horrii's face look lovely in the shadow?"

"No, Phyllis-san, it does not."

My exasperated, "WHY NOT??????"

"Phyllis-san, you must understand. Japanese people believe all things are equal."

"So?"

Equally exasperated with me, he says, "So everything must have equal illumination."

And then, finally, I get it. How obvious. Traditional Japanese art is two dimensional—that was a big clue. How could we not know? How could he not tell us? No wonder this trip is so hard.

Horii very nicely held Michael's picture for me.
Maybe we both learned something that day.

Epilogue

These many years later, this was one of the most
important moments of my life:

**The moment I understood all we do not
understand about each other. And all we
think we do. It is sad. And it is scary.**

# MY CULTURAL CONFUSION
## KENYA

### Young Maasai Warrior

(Adapted with permission by the author from the
web site: www.maasaiinfoline.org)

In case you don't know: The Maasai people of East
Africa live in southern Kenya and northern
Tanzania along the Great Rift Valley on semiarid
and arid lands. They are a semi-nomadic, pastoral
people who live under a communal system.

Livestock such as cattle, goats, and sheep are the primary source of income and food.

Until recently theirs was a cashless society.

Maasai homesteads are arranged in a circular fashion and usually shared by more than one family. The social organization of the Maasai is based on age sets, such as the warrior, bride and elder. Each have distinct roles.

Women are responsible for making the houses as well as supplying the water, collecting firewood, milking cattle and cooking for the family.

Warriors are in charge of the society's security, while boys are responsible for herding livestock.

The elders are directors and advisors for the day-to-day activities.

The spiritual leader of the tribe is the laibon.

# ME AND THE LAIBON
## JULY 1981

He was everything I expected a laibon to be. A man with presence. Mount Kilimanjaro was named after one of his ancestors—not a small thing. His village was out in the desert. I always think of it as north, but it was undoubtedly south.

Clearly, real writers' fact-check things like this.

It was a place at the end of many, many dirt roads, surrounded by acacia trees and sand all the way to the horizon.

Today there were seven of us, talent, cameraman, soundman, gaffer, two drivers, and me. I'm the director, and the boss. We arrive hot and sweaty with four flat tires among our two Jeeps.

The sun is setting, we are tired and cranky. We have been crisscrossing Kenya for weeks now and each of us desperately needs some time alone.

The count so far is one (female) talent and three affairs. Two crew members, plus the snake wrangler who took us hunting for black mambas and spitting cobras. What a fun trip that was. I guess recreational sex is a better way to put it but getting into the van every morning to see who is now cuddling who is a surprise I can live without.

Ten days earlier, we had filmed in a Maasai village much closer to Nairobi, and it had become a dangerous event. I'd been advised to offer a goat in return for permission to film life in the village.

After a morning of shooting, the young warriors offered to show us their spear skills, but only if we agreed to an additional goat. Saying yes unleashed a dangerous excitement about this new and easy source of livestock.

Too quickly the spears were flying perilously close to the cameraman's head. We left in a hurry, almost a panic. Obviously, I am inexperienced and criminally naïve when it comes to cultural chasms.

And so, I had been told in no uncertain terms by my crew that they would not shoot in this remote village until I had negotiated a flat fee for shooting—none of this goat-by-goat stuff. Too dangerous.

By now it is clear we are spending the night in the village and filming tomorrow. But first we negotiate. What could I offer the laibon in return for the pictures we wanted? My new plan was to offer a cow, maybe two. When the laibon found out he would have to negotiate with me, my plan fell apart. He was dumbfounded.

According to everything he knew, the person in charge is the eldest—my 60-year-old gaffer, John Brown. Even worse, I'm a girl. End of story.

Oh, but those cows. Long after dark, I'm asked to sneak out into the desert where no one can see us.

There's no moon. It's a starry, starry night. That scene in The Little Prince with the acacia trees and a sky full of stars comes to mind. After the plane crash, remember?

You get the idea. Basically magical.

So here we are, the laibon and me crouched in the desert with only a translator. The white and red markings on his face framing his piercing eyes cut through the dark. Damn intimidating.

And so it goes:

Him: You must never, ever tell anyone about this. It's impossible that I'm talking to you and not the old guy. He is the elder, anyone can see this.

Me: I promise.

Him: It will cost at least a second cow, maybe a few goats, too. But I will make no decision about that tonight.

Me: Please tell the laibon we would very much like to film the warriors, but we must decide the cost tonight. I can only agree if we have settled on a flat rate for all filming.

Him: It's cow by cow or nothing

Me: It's flat rate or nothing.

Him: Cow by cow. (A translator is no longer needed)

Me: Flat rate.

Etc. Etc. A half dozen rounds at least.

I am firm only because I have no choice. Inside I am quivering. We have both made our positions clear. Stalemate. And then the translator asks me if I have any booze. I travel with a bottle of brandy that he helps me retrieve from the Jeep. The laibon finishes the bottle—there is only a swig—and then tells the translator to ask me if he can keep the bottle.
Why, I ask?

The laibon has never owned a bottle, and it is a powerful place to store his medicine.

Of course, I say.

On one condition.

And what is the condition, asks the laibon?
The laibon must think of me every time he uses it.

Silence. And then laughter erupts. His laugh. In the dark, I can feel the tension melt.

Of course, he will think of you the translator says. How is it possible you have a 60-year-old son? You are in charge and so John Brown must somehow be your son, the translator patiently explains.

And how is it possible the laibon is even talking to a woman about important things like cows? If there is one thing I know, the laibon will always remember you.

These many years later I wonder if he does. Surely, he no longer has the bottle but the memory... yes. Yes, it is seared on my brain, too.

Translator: The laibon has agreed to the test. It amazes me, says the translator, but here we are.

Me: The test?

Translator: You will look into each other's eyes. Whoever turns away first...

I know this test and suck at it. Have I ever won? How can I possibly win now?

And so we stare.

His eyes are rheumy. I hadn't noticed. They are iron. He has won this test many times and will many times again. I will lose. We have come all this way and spent all this money, and I will lose.

Where is Gloria Steinem when I need her? (It is 1981 after all).

I MUST not flinch. NOT. FLINCH.

Three days pass, maybe four. A decade perhaps. Our eyes are still locked.

Gloria, Gloria... help me hang on. For women everywhere I need to do this. Ow. Are my eyeballs bleeding yet?

## And then, the laibon looks away.

# MY CULTURAL CONFUSION
# TORNADOES
## Moore, Oklahoma May 3, 1999

**May 8, 1999:** The Great Plains Tornado Outbreak was the largest outbreak in Oklahoma's history, with reports of more than 70 twisters. "One of these funnels entered Moore from the west and promptly flattened several clusters of homes. It remains the strongest known tornado in the world, with winds that reached up to 318 m.p.h. (Rated EF5)"

It was part of an unprecedented outbreak that Monday evening and afternoon, one of 14 tornadoes produced by a supercell thunderstorm. In all, 44 people lost their lives.

In 2000 Ward and Associates was contacted by The Weather Channel to document this storm and explain the incredible power of tornadoes to their audience.

It was an hour that explored the science of tornadoes, interspersed with dramatic human stories. My specialty.

**THE FIRST:** The fire chief of Moore stood on the rooftop of his station and told me how he watched helplessly as the tornado approached his home. His family was safe, but he described its total destruction in just moments, happening before his very eyes, as he watched. It was a powerful story.

I thank him and then Gino, my cameraman of many decades, says, uh, Phyllis... uh, I forgot to turn on the audio. YOU WHAT?????

The fire chief told me his story again, this time with much less fervor. Full of AS I SAID... and AS YOU KNOW. Serves me right for not hiring a sound man.

**THE SECOND:** Darlene invites us into her living room in her rebuilt home. Behind her sofa is a piece of two-by-four framed on black velvet. This is her story.

When the tornado came, Darlene and her daughter climbed into a closet for safety.

After the storm passed, she came out of the closet to discover a four-foot-long piece of a two-by-four embedded in her carotid artery.

Luckily, she didn't panic. Her daughter ran to the neighbors to get help. They brought a pickup and gently lifted Darlene into the back of the truck bed and drove her to the hospital.

Miraculously, they extracted it. And here is part of it behind me, she says. Wow.

I found video pictures of Darlene getting into the truck, and trust me when I tell you, it was scary.

And so, being the hot-shit interviewer that I am, I ask, Darlene, "What were you thinking as they lifted you into the truck?"

Well, Phyllis, she says to me. The truth is that I had gained a few pounds over the holidays and was embarrassed about my weight.

Huh???? Yes, that is exactly what the woman told me

If ever I do a special on women and their body image, it will start with this clip and Darlene's embarrassment. Really?

**THE THIRD:** We are talking to Thomas. A nine-year-old Black child who has that amazing nine-year-old man/boy ability to bring you into his world as if you were in the room with him.

When the tornado barreled down on his house he was in the bathtub. His mom and baby sister were covering him.

When it was over, they were both dead.

He described this as if it was a movie. Every terrifying moment. It was one of the most powerful interviews of my life. I asked what the worst part was.

I killed them, he said.

You killed them? How did you do that, Thomas?

After school, my mom told me to come inside and do my homework. I was playing with my friends and didn't want to come. I yelled at her and said I wish you were dead. I killed them.

He started to cry. He hadn't told anyone this before. It became a riveting segment of television. All of us who worked on it were very, very proud. We had worked together for over 20 years and to a person—camera, editor, associate producer—felt it was one of the best of our lives.

And, even better, Thomas would now start to talk to the people who could help. So we went back to DC, cut it together into an hour of what we thought was great television, and sent it to Atlanta for approval.

This was 2001 and my husband Michael and I finally moved into our home on the Eastern Shore of Virginia. It took us a while to get used to the quiet—no car alarms honking, no wailing ambulances, no sweet smell of marijuana wafting through the air ---all replaced by the hoot of owls in the dark and the early morning sounds of egrets and crab boats on the Chesapeake Bay. At 9:20 on a beautiful Monday morning, The Weather Channel called.

As a good executive producer, my boss started his phone call with compliments.

There is some immensely powerful material here, Phyllis.

Thanks very much, says I. We are proud of this piece here at Ward and Associates.
I love the fire chief telling his story, says he. Love it. And Darlene is great, too. But that video you have of the two-by-four stuck in her neck has to go. It's just too graphic.

Okay, I say, disappointedly. Okay.

Now for Thomas. You need to drop the whole story.

HUH? I must have heard you wrong. Drop the entire story? Why? We think it's one of our best stories ever. Thomas is so vulnerable and so in the present.

I totally agree, says Mr. EP. He is amazing. I was totally moved.

So, what's the problem?

Phyllis, I thought you knew. Nobody dies on The Weather Channel.

NOBODY DIES? I had no idea.

He assumed I knew. To him it was axiomatic. To me it was breaking news.

How could we have so misunderstood each other? Why would he have hired me, knowing that personal interviews are what I do best? Was there a handbook I didn't get?

I was simply devastated.

When we hung up, I went out and sat on my steps into the bay and sobbed. Just sobbed.

The thought of telling my folks in DC that what they considered some of their best work was cut... ugh.

And then my eagle flew by, and the sun was bouncing off the water... and I realized that in the scope of the planet this was a very small thing.

It mattered to me, but the rest of the world didn't really care. It was yet **another cultural misunderstanding.**

Two well intentioned people who both spoke English, both grew up in America, and both totally failed to communicate what to each of them, was a basic truth.

To this day nobody dies on The Weather Channel, not up close and personal. Total number of deaths are reported, but that's all.

At that moment, sitting alone on the bay, I realized I was done with Television. Or it was done with me. We never pitched another documentary. It took a year or so to wind down. I shot a few interviews for 20/20 or Entertainment Tonight, but never again pitched a long form documentary of our own.

## NOBODY DIES ON THE WEATHER CHANNEL

**was my tipping point.**

# AND SO... In Conclusion

When I was younger "Does It Scare Me?" was my criteria for taking a project. If it doesn't, it's not worth doing, I thought. Geez. Great way to go on adventures though. And I got to live my life going wide and deep into the places my curiosity led me. Such a privilege.

The highlights were hanging around in so many different cultures assuming I understood what was going on around me and not knowing a damn thing. We are so egocentric, aren't we?

As I think you've gathered by now, I'm a leftover hippie and die-hard feminist, who was determined to save the world. How did that work out, huh?

It's a job way too big for most of us. But I tried to do my part. So many of my documentaries were intended to shine a light into a dark corner, hoping to get your attention, hoping it would lead to change. A half a dozen of them did. I am very proud of them. Very proud. Not change just because of me, mind you, but a light that added slowly to a tipping point. Some are still waiting. Have you noticed yet how sssllllooowwww change happens?

As much as life has a point, I hope mine does. A few years ago, I decided that the point of anyone's life is, really, just to amuse ourselves. Sounds impossibly selfish, doesn't it?

As for us individuals, the research says (one last factoid) most people are remembered for three generations. Yep, that's it. Okay, if you're Plato or Jesus, or George Washington you hang around longer. Not to say we're not wonderful, and not to say we each shouldn't do our part, but let's be sure that whatever we're doing amuses us, too. BIG insight of mine a few years ago. Got rid of a lot of hippie guilt.

Since then, I've realized that most of what amuses me also tries to make the world a better place. I also realize I'm speaking from a place of great privilege. It's not amusing to struggle every day to feed your family or live in pain. I'm a spoiled woman with a Capital M marriage, a career of many adventures (if not quite Capitol C, I had a Capitol A for Adventures), and still no kids, with no regrets.

As for these snippets, I have written them to share with you the adventures of invisible ones, the ones decidedly off-camera, doing our best to shine those flashlights into dark corners, or just bring you silly stories. JUMPCUTS galore.

# Yes, Moe, it is a long story. Oh well.

# Thanks for reading.

# EPILOGUE

# CAKEBUCKS

## Wanna know how successful I was in television?
## May I present Ckebucks.

So, what's a Cakebuck? It started with a mislaid letter that was finally delivered to me three years after it was sent. It came to me from the Producers and Writers Guild of America, telling me I had a pension coming and they have been unable to find me.

7/27/18

Dear PWGA,

The enclosed letter reached me yesterday.

What a nice surprise.

Thank you to your intrepid researcher.

I'm enclosing a copy of my passport

I will get this in the mail today—it arrived

yesterday—and will also call you.

Thanks so much, Phyllis Ward

Such a nice surprise, pension money I knew nothing

about. I have no memory of being in this guild, but

apparently I was. For some projects, I automatically

enrolled, I guess.

I know I'm in the Director's Guild, 'cause I paid

them real money in dues each year and in return,

each year they send me movie screeners for the

DGA Best Director awards.. It's a terrific benefit.

But PWGA was a nice surprise.

I assume most members get big money in their

pension for their big time work. Not that it's likely

that people like Steven Speilberg and Spike Lee

need it of course, but  still. I knew I wasn't looking

at $30,000 a month.

I sent off the letter and waited.

| | THIS PERIOD |
|---|---|
| | $75.67 |
| | 0.00 |
| | 0.00 |
| | |
| | $75.67 |

Nine days later, a check showed up for $75.67. And apparently it will come once a month for the rest of my life. If Michael is still alive, he can collect half of that until he dies. That $37.83 isn't much, but hey.

The check was thrilling. Totally unexpected money. All mine. No need to share. Michael agreed. Hard-earned. When it comes every month, we convert it to cash, and I put it in my Cakebucks stash. That's the word my friend Debbie invented to describe money that unexpectedly shows up—in the couch cushions, in an old jacket pocket, that quarter you find on the street, and the referral fee you thought would never happen. Cakebucks.

MUST be spent on me and things I wouldn't otherwise buy. Truffle oil for French fries, that adorable sweater on sale I don't need, a guilt-free fig-scented candle. No need to feel guilty or ask Michael. Cakebucks to the rescue. No questions asked. And $75.67 is just enough to buy drinks for three friends at our favorite hangout. They call to see what I'm up to around the first of the month... just checking in, they say. Cakebucks are glorious.

CAKEBUCKS. Thanks, Debbie.

# Photo credits

## Unless otherwise noted all pictures belong to the author or are in public domain

Pg. 37 Heart graphic Flickr DSC00134 Jordan Thevenow-Harrison

Pg. 47 lottery numbers Ruay Santeri Vinamaki © by-SA 4.0

Pg. 51 photographs Evelyn and Frederic © Bonnet House archives

Pg. 54 Exterior of Bonnet House © David Warren Photography

Pg. 56 room of Frederic and Evelyn Paintings © Sandy Dolan

Pg. 57 Bonnet House Courtyard © Sandy Dolan

Pg. 57 Giraffe hallway, © Bonnet House archives

Pg. 58 Bonnet house living room with columns © J. Christopher Gernert

Pg. 59 Bonnet House doorway, orchid house, outdoor hallway © Bonnet House Archives

Pg.173 Manicure Isaiah Maghanga Creative Commons

Pg. 174 Cartoon © Nick Galifianakis

Pg. 195 Lily Tomlin illustration Maurice Spector

Pg. 197 James DePreist © Oregon Symphony

Pg. 203 .James DePreist © Oregon Symphony

Pg. 210 Itzhak Pearlman and James DePreist © Oregon Symphony

Pg. 229 My Attitude illustration © Maurice Spector

Pg. 231 Bench under tree © Carmen Fields

Pg. 258 Man's face © Brian Kaiser

Pg. 269 Katarina Witt Wikimedia Commons by cooperation with the German Federal Archive

Pg. 311 Eagle © Doug Spiro

I have repeatedly done my best to contact copyright holders. Please contact me to correct any errors.

# ACKNOWLEDGEMENTS

I have done my best to write a truthful story. JUMPCUTS reflects my present memories of experiences over decades. Some names have been omitted, and some dialogue has been recreated.

The list of people to thank grows every day. Claudia Bagwell, Brian Kaiser, and Ann Hayden who each kicked my butt into writing these stories down. I think they got tired of hearing them. This book wouldn't exist without them.

Claudia tediously and patiently taught me I know nothing about apostrophes. Brian heroically formatted the raw manuscript and held my hand through way too many technical difficulties. He is a kind man. Ann always had a wise opinion. All of them stayed on my case.

Karen Gravelle's sharp comments, careful reviews, and constant enthusiasm were perfect.

Moe Spector gets the first sentence and the last, of course. And he illustrated all five of my **Words To Live By**.

Kevin Stawieray's many skills created the cover design.

Barbara Ellis-Uchino was an unexpected gift who helped format the words on the page. Tim Smith and Laurie Rackas were so encouraging.

Most of all thanks to all of you long-suffering people who lived these stories with me. Oh, we had fun. Except when we didn't. So often on the ride back from so many shoots, my mantra was "Other than that Mrs. Lincoln, how was the play?"

Gino Bruno, cameraperson, was my second husband for decades. Craig Gibson, you never dropped your donut.

Kevin Cloutier I could listen to you all day. I did. For months..

Peter, Nick, Bobby and John what adventures we had. And what wonderful things you Brits taught me.

Yvonne McGee you are a talented and patient editor. I searched everywhere for a picture of you at work, to no avail. Damn it.

Doug Spiro you are in so many of these stories doing the unsung work of making television happen. I've had so many great associate producers in my life, and I thank every one of you. Doug you are one of the greats.

Thanks to Melvyn Smith and Oscar Welch who gave me my first oh-so-memorable day in television.

And of course, long-suffering Michael. He's still getting used to having me home all the time. Poor guy.

# ABOUT THE AUTHOR

Phyllis Ward began her working life as a college teacher, and a well-traveled educational consultant. Then a public school teacher and media director for a small school district. Then media director for a psychiatric hospital. Then television seduced her.

Ward began her television career as a producer/director/writer in Washington, DC, Baltimore, and London. After starting her own production company, she traveled the country and the world for 25 years, making films for just about every network out there—and meeting lots of incredible people along the way. And lots of non-profits, too. "We worked for anybody with the not so big bucks to hire us." She is most proud of winning a Dupont-Columbia Journalism Award in 1985 for a documentary she produced on the baby boom generation and its continuing effects on American life.

Ward lives with her husband Michael on the Eastern Shore of Virginia. Now retired from her second career in real estate, she spends her time enjoying this magical place and writing the occasional snippet.

Below are a few of the dozens of awards Ward and Associates won. We can't find the list anymore. We found a few of these in the laundry room and hope you will take our word about the rest.

Made in the USA
Monee, IL
14 February 2023

27204829R00190